praise for

Degrees of Failure

Most students today have given up on the utopian dreams of earlier generations and now simply seek certification in order to gain access to what are
often disappointing, precarious jobs. This, in turn, has meant deteriorating
working conditions for professors, researchers, and instructors whose hopes
for critical thinking and creativity in their classrooms have largely been replaced by pragmatism, fierce individualism, and efficiency. Under these circumstances, Randle Nelsen advocates for innovative approaches to higher
education, replacing schooling with education and credentialism with critical thinking and analysis. For Nelsen, it's time to re-embrace creativity and
return to the promise of C.W. Mills' sociological imagination.
— Norene Pupo, professor of sociology, York University

A thought-provoking analysis of the post-secondary education system in
North America. Randy Nelsen blends personal experience in the sector
with wide-reading and critical research to reflect on the impact of commercialization, technology, and an increasingly managerial culture on the traditional goals of universities in developing and fostering the exchange of
knowledge. He makes a convincing argument that these might be reclaimed by prioritizing the interests of students, through problem-based
learning, and by closer engagement with the wider community.
— Stephen McBride, professor of political science, McMaster
University, and author of *Working? Employment Policy in Canada*

Having written about higher education since before most current students' parents were students themselves, Nelsen brings a much needed long memory to the work of identifying and understanding the key socio-historical trends shaping higher education. For students, professors, staff, or anyone interested in ensuring quality education within our post-secondary institutions, this new book is unsettling.

> — Scott Thompson, assistant professor of sociology, University of Saskatchewan

Once again Nelsen has outdone himself. Not only is this text accessible, he keeps it pertinent in the academic sense as he methodically carves the university and college system into its multi-faceted business-based pieces. He has put into print what I have believed for years as I have watched my universities treat me like a consumer instead of a student, and then as a "checkout boy" instead of a teacher. This work stands as, not a cry, but a scream for change, and I hope it fuels the debate to an explosive end.

> — Dr. Stephen E. Bosanac, Department of Sociology, York University

As universities tempt potential students and donors with glossy marketing tools and pundits suggest that youth without degrees have bleak futures, Randle Nelsen warns that higher education today is "a morbid mess." Fundamental educational practices have come to be displaced by priorities associated with business and commodified entertainment. Despite what has been lost, however, Nelsen reminds us that genuine education possibilities can be sustained by drawing upon transformative pedagogical practices that engage participants.

> — Terry Wotherspoon, Department of Sociology, University of Saskatchewan

Contents

Acknowledgements

Once again I have been fortunate to have Robert Clarke agree to be my editor. As I have noted before, "Rob truly is the writer behind the writer." His organizational skills and knack for stating things clearly and concisely offer a role model for me and other writers, especially those of an academic bent, to emulate. His talented persistence in getting it right always makes my work better. I am indeed thankful that, amidst carefully considered plans to scale back his busy editing schedule and devote more time to his own research and writing projects, Rob found time to edit this volume. Thanks, Rob.

I once again counted on Steve Izma to do his usual superior job of text design and page preparation. He managed to work me into his busy schedule in a timely manner. Thanks, Steve.

I want to give special acknowledgement to the efforts of Between the Line's managing editor, Amanda Crocker, who gave strong support to this project. I very much appreciated the effectiveness and dispatch with which she tackled problems and cleared the way for this book's publication. Her pleasing disposition and solid efficiency were also to be found in abundance among all the BTL staff, who as a group took away my production worries and replaced them with supportive confidence. It has been a pleasure to work with you, and I thank you all.

Finally, I recognize that it would be extremely difficult to acknowledge everyone who has contributed something to the ideas and analysis found in this book. My thoughts on many of the matters discussed have been developing for half a century, and the probability of leaving out important contributors runs high. However, I do want to offer a general acknowledgement to those close to me for their loving support and inspiration, for the foundation they provided. To my friends and family in Hamilton, Thunder Bay, Montreal, Portland, and elsewhere, while I have not named you individually, please be assured that this book could not have been completed without you by my side. Thanks for your unwavering support and for having my back.

R.W. Nelsen, May 2017

ONE

The University from the Inside-Out

Thoughts of a Participant Observer

T he state of higher education today is in a morbid mess. Our colleges and universities are edubusiness corporations that operate on business principles and are managed by administrators who serve the interests of wealthy capitalists. Yet this world of corporate higher education – constructed by the rich, who disguise their interests as philanthropy – is by no means a recent phenomenon. Its history has unfolded in the United States and Canada over the past two-hundred-plus years. The consequences are many and varied, and all participants, regardless of their position within or connection to the university hierarchy – faculty, students, parents, support staff and/or service workers, and even administrators themselves – pay the price.

Members of university faculties are increasingly attuned to the reward structure sponsored by the philanthropists, who treat the teaching staff as lobbyists who can be bought and sold. As faculty members chase after privatized research funding and government-sponsored grants, they accordingly reduce the amount of time spent on classroom preparation and being present in the classroom. The emphasis in their work is necessarily on research. The consultant-grants-person professors have little opportunity to model scholarly curiosity and inquiry; the students are left with a professorial model of vapid professionalism buttressed by high-tech electronic-based learning that helps ensure a classroom experience that reproduces rather than challenges status quo arrangements.

For the most part, the students are not to blame for this mess. They are its unfortunate victims or casualties. Just to adapt and survive they have to rationally shift their own thinking and priorities. They tend to view themselves as consumers of education who are seeking certification legitimacy by obtaining academic degrees and professional licences to practise. For many students, emulating their professor role models, the university system has become a game to be beaten or scammed; more traditional scholarly orientation gives way to jumping educational hurdles not unlike the challenges of the various levels in the video games they have grown up with. The high-tech classroom becomes just another part of the students' immersion in the familiar world of electronic social media. It is a learning environment that greases the slide into edutainment and away from scholarship.

Parents join students in the practical understanding that certification through higher education is an expensive and time-consuming process. With tuition fees and the general cost of living (room, board, and other expenses) rising, many students are forced to work part-time, a lesser number full-time, and almost all parents are called upon to contribute financially in some way. Most significantly, parents are justifiably worried about their children's futures in a struggling economy that features the uncertainty of precarious labour. Some parents (referred to as "helicopter parents") become overprotective as they try to chaperone their children through this certification process, often causing increased anxiety and strain on both parties, as well as leading to unnecessary classroom protections that hinder scholarly exchange and further emphasize the edutainment aspect of higher education.

Administrators, continually on the prowl for more funding to do their benefactors' bidding, contribute to creating the edutainment learning environment. Big-time college sports play an outsized role in attracting alumni and wealthy benefactor dollars, and I outline in some detail how this has worked out at the University of Oregon. Administrators at various major universities not only oversee but encourage the party atmosphere of game-day Saturdays with their attendant tailgates as the party moves from the playing fields and stadium parking lots to classrooms grounded on edutainment. At the same time they are overseeing the cutting of full-time faculty positions alongside a dramatic rise in the use and abuse of part-time sessional faculty. Meanwhile the ranks of administrators charged with recruiting funds and various bookkeeping tasks continue to grow.

Somewhat bizarrely in this world of supposed higher learning, its members – students, teachers, parents, university support staff, and service workers – have at least one thing in common: cars and the need for a valid parking sticker that allows for easy access to and exit from today's increasingly commuter-oriented institutions. With all the off-campus jobs, the need for classroom attendance (when classes are not online), and research and funding recruitment appointments, the necessarily frequent trips back and forth to the college or university learning boutique are not unlike consumer activity at the nearby shopping centre or mall. A road-worthy car and a space to conveniently park it are essential elements of the educational environment. The automobile is also the centrepiece for the tailgate parties accompanying the college sports spectacles that are an integral part of higher education's edutainment focus. With the tailgates and campus commutes as obvious examples, automobility and today's universities become "third places" tightly connected to the two other social spaces that are primary to all of us: family and work.

If the automobile is a key technology in college and university learning experiences, computer-based electronic-learning technology is another – something that has reshaped the classroom and scholarship in general in its image. In the movement towards computer-mediated online education at a distance, the institution where I teach, Lakehead University in Thunder Bay, with the sociology department as a case in point, provides several examples of what has been transpiring in this regard.

While the increasing power of electronic-based social media to shape and control our lives extends beyond the university, it is the learning context of the classroom that especially interests me. Indeed, to a certain extent *social media* is a misnomer. Often these media can be characterized as anti-social, and perhaps undemocratic as well. For instance, Sherry Turkle, a clinical psychologist and professor of the social studies of science and technology at the Massachusetts Institute of Technology (MIT), argues that computer technology, rather than bringing us together, is making us "alone together," and she urges us to reclaim conversation, to save it from the technology to which we have become addicted.[1] Scholarship is certainly a social activity – or at least it should be – and Turkle's work has important ramifications and implications when it comes to organizing the university classroom as a learning environment.

How, then, can we go about reorganizing and reshaping college classrooms in order to make them more user-friendly? And by "user-friendly" I mean everything from architectural design to, most especially, the development of course content with students included in the planning process as a top priority – basically, a student-centred as opposed to the teacher- or professor-centred approach that continues to be dominant in universities (with classrooms organized to service the desires, needs, and interests of the professors). One first step is to make storytelling a major focal point in reconstructing the classroom environment. An emphasis on sharing and learning from each other's stories can provide a learning context that is less structured by bureaucratic authority relations and can introduce more opportunities for the classroom to be student-centred. The classroom becomes open to the wider community outside the university, and the wider community to the university. Storytelling can form an effective combination with project work: that is, student projects or research work that go beyond the standard library-oriented term paper and reach out to contact and connect university classrooms with members of the surrounding community. A user-friendly classroom would have the additional advantage of reducing the dependence on technology. Storytelling and other possibilities emphasize the importance of returning to more in-person instruction in a classroom in which learners can meet regularly face to face, preferably in a seminar format – an arrangement that has several advantages over, and is superior to, Massive Open Online Courses (MOOCs), which, at many colleges and universities, have been fast-tracked as the preferred method of instruction to be celebrated in our electronic age.

Storytelling as a primary focus in our university classrooms not only brings history into our contextual understandings but also, in so doing, encourages us to think of our present circumstances in terms of the legacy that we will leave future generations. Storytelling also puts a premium upon listening skills, something that today's students and all of us, in an age of preoccupation with rapid-fire social media and the assertion of self, need to work on developing and refining. Stories can help to create an atmosphere in which diversity and inclusion are not only tolerated but encouraged.

In all of this we have much to learn from Indigenous peoples and their oral culture of storytelling. As Naomi Klein outlines in her book *This Changes Everything: Capitalism vs. the Climate*, Indigenous experiences reveal tried and true ways of creating and sustaining a more just and environmentally sustainable society.[2] Storytelling can be very powerful, with a great potential for helping to initiate social change. The advantages of storytelling in a seminar format will stay with our college and university students long after they graduate. I hope that this book might occasion reflection upon how to safeguard, nurture, and use our stories. They offer building blocks for reflection, adaption, and change, providing opportunities to consider and create improved alternatives to what is.

On Method: Interpretation, C. Wright Mills, and Stories

Social analysis – like storytelling – involves interpretation. This book contains material that sociologists might label and refer to as "hard data," along with references to academic books and journals. It also contains references to informed journalism in popular literary and current affairs magazines that I find helpful in exploring the connections between individual consciousness and collective social arrangements – or in considering the affinity between ideas and socio-historical trends in higher education. Like other social analysts, I draw upon my own experience, in this case fifty-five years of university experience as a student, both undergraduate and graduate, and professor. As a result the book contains elements of what today's students of sociology and cultural studies would call "autoethnography" as I examine and interpret several events by weaving together autobiography and social context.[3] Given my familiarity with the terrain of sociology, my critique of professionals and their training as experts often features that discipline as "a whipping boy," as exemplifying the deleterious consequences of a corporatized and professionalized higher learning. Yet my goal always is to fulfill what C. Wright Mills called the "task" and "promise" of "the sociological imagination [that] enables us to grasp history and biography and the relations between the two within society."[4]

Crucial in the development of this imagination is interpretation. Because we humans are social animals who weave complex and complicated connections and relationships, interpretation is always at the centre of analyses of our social interactions. Furthermore, the interconnections between people's ideas and their social arrangements indicate that many questions and issues of concern to social analysts cannot be answered by studies where "the details are piled up with insufficient attention to form," what Mills called "abstracted empiricism."[5] For sociologists and others in the social sciences, the details or "facts" are social, which means that they come to social investigators already interpreted. Analysts then, whether or not they self-identify as scientists, are faced with accepting the analytic reality that they, like the individuals and groups they study, live in a socio-historical institutional framework with others rather than in another and different world of abstractions. In addition, control by the analyst, even when it is desired, over the social groups and data that make up our subject matter is always problematic. Control over our data can never be complete – a point that is similar and connectible to a key argument in this book: namely, that the best way to reorganize our classrooms in order to create a more hospitable and effective learning environment is to give up a sizeable measure of professorial control.

When ethnography and social analysis meet and inform each other, as I hope is the case here, interpretation is both informed by and deeply reliant on memory; and memories are often imperfect. Memory is "a holding cell," a phrase that Canadian humorist and award-winning novelist Will Ferguson employs to describe the recollections of individuals.[6] It is a phrase that can also be applied to cultural subgroups and whole cultures as a description of communal, or collective, recollections. Memory and interpretation are both closely connected to ideology, a term that is used not only in reference to individuals, often to address the "false consciousness" of those who are not aware of their true role, but also to signify the consciousness of an epoch. My analytic focus here is on indicating our epoch's limitations, the manner in which social interaction is imposed and regulated by the affinity between thought forms and social structure with regard to higher education. I take my lead from renowned linguist and social justice activist Noam Chomsky, who writes about the connection between science and ideology and the ever-present potential for one to turn into the other: "When we consider the responsibility of intellectuals, our basic concern must be their role in the creation and analysis of ideology."[7]

Ideology, then, can be correctly viewed as having a reciprocal effect as it moves between and is influenced by human interactions that connect people and issues both to the larger social context and to the collective consciousness of those working within specific academic disciplines such as sociology and history. Thus, philosophers of science speak about and examine an ideology of science, and similarly sociologists have a branch specialization known as the sociology of sociology – a subfield that informs some of my commentary in the following pages. The well-known work of Thomas Kuhn is relevant as he speaks to how prevailing paradigms in academic fields are shaped and shifted, a social process that eventually reaches a tipping point whereby practitioners achieve a consensus on a new paradigm that replaces the old.[8] Ideology, interpretation, sociology, and, of course, the structural relations of power – all play their parts as we go about the daily business of deconstructing and reconstructing the "facts," discourses, and interpretations that form the basis of our understandings. The metahistory work of historian Hayden White also frames my thinking regarding method and approaches: White examines how we employ different modes of emplotment, argument, and ideological implication in constructing the narratives of our lives individually and collectively.[9]

In living my life, and especially in my role as an analyst, I attempt to recognize and acknowledge the ways in which ideological underpinnings may combine with cultural discourses (academic paradigms included) in the developing narratives I construct. The kind of sociology I do, the present work included, has always leaned towards the historical and what I consider the most primary and demanding task of unmasking complex relations of power. Over the years I have found that literature and a kind of investigative journalism, in the tradition of muckrakers such as Ida M. Tarbell and Upton Sinclair, are complementary fields that often provide keen sociological insights.[10] The infamous Chicago School of Sociology that emerged during the 1920s and 1930s owes a good part of its foundation and notoriety to former journalist-turned-sociologist Robert Park. This school produced several well-known participant-observation studies that share the same spirit with and are in part forerunners of today's autoethnographies.[11] The best work in this tradition gives due consideration to both structure and agency. Like history written from the bottom up, it attempts to uncover the standpoints of all the actors, regardless of their position in the structures of authority and power. The goal is to reveal as much as possible about their structural positioning and the values, beliefs, and motives that, taken together, show where they stand in the confluence of personal concerns and social issues. Relevant background interests and biographical information revealing the standpoint of the social analyst should also be part of the analysis. In trying to construct my version of standpoint analysis, I take my lead from Dorothy E. Smith, who, in several writings elaborating upon her creation of "standpoint sociology," advocates practising a sociological analysis that draws upon and reaffirms the experiences of women.[12]

Mills and the sociological analyses he constructs can also help us to gain further insights regarding the effectiveness of combining sociology and journalism in the art of storytelling. In the latter part of his short career, prior to his untimely death in 1964, Mills turned more and more towards journalistic storytelling in applying his sociological sensibilities and talents to pressing social issues. His wisdom and warnings are to be found in books such as *The Causes of World War Three* and *Listen, Yankee: The Revolution in Cuba*. In *Listen, Yankee* he wrote and spoke from his travel and living experiences in Cuba about the revolution there as well as revealing to Americans, for those who cared to listen, the complicated and ongoing struggles of all the Latin American countries in general. In doing so Mills never lost sight of what was in his view "perhaps the most fruitful distinction with which the sociological imagination works" – the distinction between "the personal troubles of milieu" and "the public issues of social structure."[13] He argued that classical sociologists have left us a tradition demanding that intellectual problems be made relevant to the public issues of the times and the private troubles of individual men and women: the "sociological imagination" they practised "enables us to grasp history and biography and the relations between the two within society."[14] My hope is that this book will help readers carry this approach further with respect to higher education in Canada and the United States.

TWO

Campus Parking and the Car as a Third Place

Asphalt Grievances and Commuter Sociability

I n 1964 – more than fifty years ago – Clark Kerr, as chancellor of the massive University of California system, described the growth of the modern multiversity as "a series of individual faculty entrepreneurs held together by a common grievance over parking."[1] Although Kerr undoubtedly meant his statement to be humorous, today it is well past time to remove tongue from cheek when it comes to parking and day-to-day university life. Parking has become *a*, some would say *the*, major policy item in university planning. While it might seem odd or almost out of place to begin a book on higher education with a chapter about cars, the issues of automobility and colleges/universities – and especially on-campus parking, both the lack and expansion of it – are inextricably linked.[2] Not surprisingly to university insiders, "parking space" and accessibility – as we will see in the examples of three Canadian schools – play a significant role in negotiations with regard to faculty recruitment, promotion, and even retention.

Parking at McMaster, York, and Lakehead

Not so long ago a department chair at McMaster University was moved into a more senior administrative position.[3] A key negotiating piece brought to the table for this promotion was that the offer, if accepted, would guarantee the professor a conveniently located, always-available on-campus parking spot. There was none of the usual quibbling over salary, proposed occasional teaching assignments, or any other perks –

only parking, in this case with a capital P. The professor, I have since discovered, was simply taking a page out of the university president's book. One of the few committees on which the president sits is the university's parking committee.

McMaster, founded in 1887 in Toronto through a bequest from the estate of businessman-banker Senator William McMaster, is located in Hamilton, Ontario, a city of over half-a-million residents that more than doubles in size when you take the population of the surrounding metropolitan area into account. The university is about an hour's bus ride from downtown Toronto, where it was first located before moving to Hamilton in 1930. Its population of some 30,000 students (approximately three times the number in place when I first enrolled in 1970) includes about 3,700 students living on campus in twelve residences. The remaining students, close to 88 per cent of the total, can therefore be placed in the category of commuters. Some 1,400 members of the academic staff and nearly 6,500 support workers add to the mix – and the majority of them do not use public transportation. Furthermore, with the McMaster campus being decidedly more urban than rural, situated on only 152.4 hectares or 377 acres of land, parking space is at a premium. A valid campus parking sticker is clearly an important item.

In this competition for scarce spaces, the campus has more than twenty parking lots, with several of them located across a thoroughfare adjacent to the central campus – a distance great enough to call for the use of a shuttle bus. In 2015 the cost for a preferred non-commercial spot ran as high as $101 a month (HST included), although for the shuttle-bus sites the price could go down to $48 per month. If you had a motorcycle that you wanted to park, you were in luck at just $17 a month. If you participated in night-time intramural sports, your basketball jones could cost you $7 an outing if you wanted to park on campus. Better to buy a motorcycle or a scooter; it might be cheaper in the long run. As these figures indicate, financial means (the ability to pay beyond car payments, maintenance, and insurance bills), typically limited for most students, is an important sorting mechanism in determining who gets to claim a desirable on-campus parking spot. But when you have money combined with the pull of rank and status inside the institution, the task of finding a berth for your ride is greatly facilitated. Our newly appointed administrator definitely had his priorities in proper order and followed a negotiating strategy that served well in this regard.

Just up from the Queen Elizabeth Way (QEW) at York University, the situation is even more grim and alarming. The school's size and location are issues here. With some 53,000 students and 7,000 faculty and administrative staff, York is the third-largest university in Canada, behind the University of Toronto (U of T) and the University of British Columbia (UBC). Founded in 1959 and part of the Canadian postwar boom in higher education, the university opened in September 1960 on the U of T campus. It moved to its own campus, Glendon College on Bayview Ave., the next year and from there expanded, a few years later, to what would be its main campus on Keele St. in far-off North York. With a large number and variety of facilities and buildings – its York Lanes shopping mall and an array of medical services, banking, clothing, eateries, and many other options, combined with the huge population of students and university employees served – the Keele Campus became an entity resembling a mid-size city. Based on 2011 statistics on Ontario's fifty cities, the Keele Campus city and associated locations would rank in the middle, around number 28 – a mid-sized city with the bonus of a reasonably well-stocked academic bookstore.

The Keele Campus's 457 acres make it the largest post-secondary campus in Canada. Its eight undergraduate residences each house about 250 students, for a total of 2,000. Several smaller apartment complexes accommodate others. The old Glendon Campus has two residences, Hilliard and Wood, which between them have 400 beds. Accounting for some inaccuracies and incomplete data as to exactly how many people reside on-campus at York, a reasonable estimate would be that only about 7 per cent of the total student body lives there, with the other 93 per cent left to figure out how to get there and back. York is, then, a classic commuter university, with fierce competition and long waiting lists for the approximately 9,200 parking spaces provided by the university. Those spaces have various designations and benefits: reserved, unreserved, day or evening (or a combination of the two), outdoor or garage. In 2014, depending on availability, a driver could spend up to $1,676.69 (HST included) for a year's worth of garage parking. That would be top dollar. From there prices descended to $1,453.63 for day/ evening unreserved, and further down to the lowest mad-scramble unreserved price of $989.88 for those able to arrange all-evening class schedules. Here again, motorcycle ownership along with answered prayers for a mild winter might serve budget-strapped students well, because in that case reserved parking spaces could be had for just a little more, $1,065.82. Yet, just as at McMaster, the availability of preferred parking trumps the ability to pay, and waiting lists have become routine standard operating procedure.

Much, much further away – by some 1,378 kilometres or 856 miles – is Thunder Bay, Northwestern Ontario's regional metropolitan centre with a population of more than 120,000. This is the city where I spent thirty-five years as a professor at Lakehead University, a relatively small school. When I first arrived in 1976, parking was free and the undergraduate population was somewhere around 2,500, with those ranks supplemented by 100 or so graduate students and plenty of part-time evening students. The latter were mostly school teachers seeking courses for further certification (a search that would later be government-mandated) to ensure jobs and move them up the salary grid. By the time I retired in 2011 Lakehead had 8,680 students, with 7,042 registered as full-time. The Lakehead teaching staff numbered 319 full-time faculty, supported by 1,850 staff, with 715 of those holding full-time positions. The campus in Thunder Bay had accommodations for 1,436 students to reside on campus. (The university also has a mainly-commuter branch plant located in Orillia, closer to Toronto.) On-campus residents, then, comprised only somewhere between 16 and 17 per cent of the school's students, making Lakehead yet another commuter university.

Still, its smaller size and a large amount of land available for parking space – a manageable walking distance from central university buildings – make Lakehead University different from McMaster and York. Another important difference is that Thunder Bay's public transportation system is nowhere near as extensive or efficient as the public mass-transit systems found in Southern Ontario. Wait times are longer, as are many of the meandering routes that lead to the university. Students and some faculty do use public transport, but as an irregular user I found that driving a car to campus is preferable. A missed connection and a twenty-minute wait in the frigid −30 to −35°C temperatures of mid-January are nobody's idea of a picnic. Also, the parking fees are a bargain compared to the fee structures of the universities to the south. At Lakehead in 2015 a spot in one of the R (reserved) lots could be had for $348 (HST included) for twelve months, or $232 for the fall-winter academic year (relatively few courses are offered in the spring-summer sessions). Reserved permit holders do not have to worry about queuing if they find no spot immediately available because they can just move over to one of the many other spaces always available in the lower-priced G (general) parking areas ($264 full-year or $176 academic-year), which are also within easy walking distance of the university facilities.

These always available spaces are the result of a previous university president's plan to create enough parking for his dream sport and convention centre that he wanted built on recently acquired land. This attempt to have a campus home for Lakehead's successful hockey team, the apple of the president's eye, was still embroiled in backroom machinations long after city council finished debating the matter and the hockey-minded president retired. But the new spaces for vehicles coming to campus remain in place, as does the combination of administrative hierarchy and university power politics that continues to play an important role in parking matters. Some people on campus still find it strange that only the reserved lot next to the central administrative building has electrical power available for vehicle plug-ins to counter the often bone-chilling cold of Thunder Bay winters. Apparently, the university's 2015–16 financial crisis, when the board and the president ordered a 4 per cent cut for the institution as a whole, does not apply to the parking lot next to the building where the president spends his on-campus time. As for motorcyclists at Lakehead, winter applies and they receive no special rate for parking.

As a commuter university Lakehead continues, like McMaster and York, to expand even more in that direction. In March 2016 I walked the halls of two buildings on the Thunder Bay campus and engaged in a counting exercise that might be a marker indicating commuter university status and the predominance of frequent daily trips of short duration back and forth to school. I had noticed that many of the lockers available to students were not being used and decided to gather statistics in that regard. In the Braun Building, the first campus building in continual use since Lakehead Technical College became Lakehead University in 1965, two floors housed a total of 436 lockers. On the first floor, only 32 out of 146 lockers, or 22 per cent, had locks on them; on the basement floor below only 5, or less than 2 per cent, of the 290 available lockers seemed to be in use. In the Centennial Building, close to and beneath the university administrative offices, the cafeteria, and the Agora (the large, open, student-centre-type space at the heart of campus life), I counted a total of 257 lockers available, and only 36, or 14 per cent, were padlocked for use. Both buildings, then, had 726 full-length lockers available; and students were padlocking, and I assume using, only 73 or 10 per cent of them.

Some thirty years ago students did not have today's mobile online electronic libraries and internet information platforms, digital systems, and e-books. Nor was there such a pressing necessity to work part-time jobs to pay for increasingly expensive college and university educations. So the days I remember, when students applied for a locker assignment and almost all lockers were being used, are long gone. While new electronic technology has played its part, our car culture emphasizing individual automobile ownership has been, for at least the past forty years, at the centre of the commuter university's growth. Commuting to today's learning boutiques often requires long periods of time spent in a car and then, at the school or workplace end of the journey, a troublesome search for an affordable and convenient parking space.[4]

Automobility and University Life: The High-Tech or Techno-Car as a New Kind of Third Place

Ray Oldenburg's much-cited 1989 book, *The Great Good Place: Cafés, Coffee Shops, Bookstores, Bars, Hair Salons, and Other Hangouts at the Heart of a Community*, has been influential. As the subtitle announces, his book focuses on how "third places" from cafés to beauty parlors and "other hangouts" help us get through our days. His edited collection, *Celebrating the Third Place: Inspiring Stories about the Great Good Places at the Heart of Our Communities*, published in 2001, expands upon the importance of these places as neutral and fertile ground away from first places (home) and second places (work), sites in which people gather and interact. They provide informal settings that offer supportive environments conducive both to individual and community participation and well-being. Over the past twenty-five years many people have embraced Oldenburg's third-place thesis and become actively engaged in their communities through different organizations. The Project for Public Spaces is exemplary in creating and preserving these places.

Oldenburg's work stresses the hard hit taken by the typical third places of U.S. society, where social contact today continues to be further diminished, giving way to the already "overworked American virtues of individualism and privacy."[5] Significantly, these so-called virtues have been historically maintained and encouraged by an automobility that brings together superhighway networks and suburban areas available for the most part to already privileged groups – mostly white, male, and of the middle- and upper-middle classes.[6] Daniel I. Vieyra, in his studies of the architecture of American life, notes how "the automobile has literally turned the American house around." He describes the turnaround this way: "As the front yard became a small, very public auto-dominated space, the family retreated to the rear yard (often fenced in) or 'garden,' with its patio which, replacing the front porch, was usually an extension of the family room, a new informal combination parlor and dining room."[7]

Largely left out of this sea change in house use and construction were those on the low end of the individualism and privacy continuum. Already marginalized groups, such as people of colour, women, and the poor, were further marginalized. But make no mistake, we all suffered, as historian Arthur Lower makes clear in detailing the phenomenon he referred to as "the great god CAR, " which "threatened to turn us all into nomads, and his wheels, like Juggernaut, levelled every physical and psychical obstacle they met" – invading urban spaces, knocking down houses, replacing agricultural fields and orchards with straight wide roads/super highways; and "they ordained that factories for making new parts of CAR should be erected in their place."[8]

Lower's "great god CAR" and Oldenburg's "great good place" are closely connected. The independently owned bar, diner, corner store, and other typical third places have, with the rise of suburbs and compartmentalized cities, disappeared at an alarming rate. That third places are fewer and diminished is in large part attributable to our increasing reliance on the automobile. Oldenburg describes a "unifunctional" approach and design in our built environments as driven by CAR:

> The sterilized or purified neighborhoods that contain nothing but houses emerged in great number as the nation became overreliant on the automobile. "Nothing neighborhoods" came into being only because the car was counted upon to satisfy every need and desire that the home could not. Eventually our overreliance on the automobile caused a deterioration in the quality of our lives that few can ignore. Since the early- or mid-seventies, Americans have begun to develop an ambivalent attitude toward automobiles. The freeways, which are the lifelines to sterilized neighborhoods, are getting clogged, as are the lesser arteries. The air is turning foul with the hundred million pounds of carbon monoxide that cars pump into it every year. The loss of life from automobile accidents touches every citizen closely. The cost of automobiles is outrageous.[9]

Few would disagree with this assessment, linking the car as a "privatized and anti-social" means of conveyance with the suburbs (the "private compounds") that it has helped to create, and his words ring even truer some twenty-five years after he wrote them. Oldenburg does not argue that automobiles caused a unifunctional design, but he is clear in noting that they made it possible: "The facilitating principles are simple enough: 1) the car can connect all points no matter where they are located, and 2) everyone who counts has a car."[10]

The first point – the rise of suburbia alongside the development of an interstate/interprovincial network of highways – is inextricably linked to the second – the developmental concerns of differing cultures and social classes, in this case CAR as an artefact of privilege and symbol of status. The social analyst and American Studies professor Reuel Denney, in sketching the history of the car as both democratic possibility and media extension, wrote: "Sometime between 1920 and 1945, roughly, the auto had passed through a stage of its existence symbolized by the comic strip 'Gasoline Alley.' As auto, it had lost much of its old novelty as transportation; in order to retain glamor, it had to become, in differentiated forms, a kind of daily apparel."[11]

Just as apparel choices and their differing affordability are social-class markers, so too are cars – from Chevrolets to Cadillacs. Denney's sociology went deeper, not only showing how cultural capital walked hand-in-hand with monetary capital but also delving into one of his favourite themes – of how differences between amateurism and professionalism are related to class. With cars he was insightful in noting that the often lower-class youth amateurism of hot-rodder culture was perceived as a threat to the middle-class professionalism and hard-won respectability of the Detroit automakers. They and their allies at times co-opted amateur innovations to improve factory products, but they also sought to destroy the amateurs. Denney writes: "Not a few people seemed to feel, without quite saying so, that the duty of young Americans was to buy cars, not to rebuild them. To rebuild a car, it appeared, was an attack on the American way."[12] Put another way, and to incorporate a 1990s advertising pitch, to modify by messing around or tinkering with the Chevy in the backyard was to mess with capitalism, "the heartbeat of America."

Hot-rod culture is but one instance that pits the movement towards freedom, of both individuals and collectives, against corporate restraint.[13] Desire for a freedom that leads to individual prestige or status and upward mobility is for some, including Oldenburg with his third-place analysis, superseded by collective concerns. These concerns offer a window – or even a mirror – on cultural identity.

Oldenburg offers a contrasting description, drawing on the observations of anthropologist Edward T. Hall,[14] comparing the smaller-sized cars driven by the French with the standard supersized cars driven by Americans: Renaults and Citroens versus Cadillacs and Lincolns. The French are socialized from birth to smaller spaces and are willing to put up with interior spaces that Americans would see as crowded and undesirable. The French understand that "Changes in the size of automobiles . . . would have repercussions throughout the entire culture." Oldenburg elaborates:

> Because their cars are small, the French can preserve a seventy-foot-wide sidewalk along the Champs-Elysees. With large American cars, that noble avenue would become the scene of mass suicide. The French are amply rewarded for squeezing themselves into small automobiles. As a consequence the life of the street is preserved for the pedestrian, for le bistro, and for the eyes and ears. When the automobile is subdued, the street remains inviting to those who shop afoot, to those for whom the daily promenade is a cherished form of relaxation, and to those whose social life depends heavily upon the neutral ground of the sidewalk café. And, when these marvelous benefits are available without the need to drive somewhere, the car remains smaller not only in size but in importance as well.[15]

Most observers would agree that the importance of CAR to North Americans, as well as the problems it creates (note the "walkability" sales pitch offered by today's realtors), has grown steadily since the time in which Oldenburg was writing. Indeed, because of technological developments that Oldenburg could not have easily foreseen more than twenty-five years ago, the car itself has become an important third place, even though it is admittedly a place in which drivers are often still "bowling alone," to use Robert Putnum's now-popular phrase.[16] In adding the automobile to Oldenburg's list of third places, I recognize that his 1989 lament and description still hold true today: "The problem of place in America manifests itself in a sorely deficient informal public life. The structure of shared experience beyond that offered by family, job, and passive consumerism is small and dwindling."[17]

As MIT professor Sherry Turkle argues, computer technology has made it possible for us to be "alone together." The ways in which we relate to each other and think about ourselves, and our ideas about what constitutes community, have been significantly changed by internet technology. Although this thesis is now commonplace, Turkle's array of illustrative examples provokes further thought, and the general argument that she and others are elaborating and refining provides a takeoff point for viewing today's automobile as a new and different kind of third place.

Late in 2015 *The New York Times* featured an automobile article, "The Weak Spot under the Hood." Authors David Gelles, Hiroko Tabuchi, and Matthew Dolan note that "the real brains" of today's car as an operating system are in "the engine control unit, a computer attached to the side of the motor that governs performance, fuel efficiency and emissions." It seems that the new hot-rodders, the tinkerers of the manufacturers' standard models, are going to have to learn techniques for cracking open this "impregnable black box . . . the gateway to the code."[18] A central concern for the authors is the potential role of this new breed of amateur car enthusiasts in keeping the manufacturers honest. The Volkswagen Corporation's shenanigans around emissions testing are simply the latest case showing that technological "complexities create openings for automakers to game the system."[19]

That the vehicle code is an exciting new site of interest for hackers can be understood simply as the latest development in technologizing the car. Technical innovations have transformed the car as place, not only for hackers but also for the rest of us everyday motorists. We have moved from eight-track to Compact Disc players, AM to FM to Sirius radio with enough channels to meet every taste, and from car screens playing videotaped movies to digital satellite television programming with movies on demand as we roll along. In our screen-culture age nearly every entertainment desire can be fulfilled for those who can afford the most up-to-date technology (and the relative cost is continually decreasing to include more of us): talking on smartphones with speakers and hands-free devices that allow drivers to participate in the conversation; passengers texting, Skyping, and FaceTiming; kids (and adults) playing video games in the backseat while drivers, friends, or whole families listen to the latest from a diverse smorgasbord of podcasts suiting a variety of interests and tastes.

These technological developments, depending on which are used and how, are capable of making today's automobile less privatized and certainly far less of an anti-social space. As a new third place they have the potential to encourage connections to people, ideas, cultural trends, and community outside the car capsule itself. Prominent among the personal benefits noted by Oldenburg as being derived from third-place social interaction are "levelling" (a kind of smoothing out or smoothing over of status and class and occupational differences and distinctions) and the "primacy of conversation" (in cars often aroused by a podcast), a "looseness of structure" (certainly options for initiating interaction inside the modern automobile are varied), the "eternal reign of the imp of fun" (even technology-induced fun may have its merits), "novelty," and "spiritual tonic."[20] These are all third-place benefits that automobility and the car as place may foster. Certainly every car trip does not provide all or even most of these benefits, but even so the automobile clearly becomes worthy of consideration as a new and different kind of third place.

One part of this consideration entails a recognition of the social interaction fostered by new car technology available for adaptation and use during lengthy commute times prior to dealing with the troublesome issue of parking. Another part is the question of where the car is headed. For the younger generation raised on high-tech culture, the so-called "digital natives," the journey often involves colleges and universities. Understanding commuter travels to these destinations (parking hassles included) is important in considering the car, and also institutions of higher learning, through a lens that reveals the day-to-day connections between the two. The commuting digitals have company, as a renewed emphasis on certification combines with sustained encouragement of life-long learning to push the car to centre stage in its role as conveyor of adults of all ages, often busy with full-time jobs, to and from the campus. The car, then, with the university attached, has become an important third social space for many, and just as a marginalized hot-rod subculture has been marketed into the mainstream, in much the same manner "ivory tower" post-secondary education has also been mainstreamed. The commuting high-tech car brings edubusiness-sponsored edutainment to learning, influencing and shaping university life. The car helps to move entertainment from the highway to parking lots for university game-day parties – and from there into the classroom in the form of edutainment.

As an exemplar of this phenomenon, tailgate parties have in themselves become not just profitable sites for capitalist enterprise but also, most importantly, social gatherings that embody the search for sociability and community.[21] This particular party is certainly not a homogeneous community, divided as it is by intersections grounded in gender, ethnic, and most especially social-class differences,[22] but in many ways it has greater influence, a binding social influence, than the sports spectacle that occasions it, the game itself. And it is the cars or other game-day conveyances (SUVs, pickup trucks, motor homes, and so on) – the vehicles transporting family and friends to the game – that take centre stage. In the parking lot the vehicle functions as architectural host for the party. Sometimes the party can last for days, perhaps a long weekend, in parking lots quite far removed from the stadium. Clearly the social goings-on are as relevant as, and often more important than, game day and the game itself.

As I described this party context in my book *Fun & Games & Higher Education: The Lonely Crowd Revisited*, "In The Grove at Ole Miss, outside Oregon's Autzen Stadium, at Dartmouth's Memorial Field – in every region of the country – autumn Saturdays mean participation in a festival-like community recreated not only from one weekend to the next but from one generation to the next."[23] Based upon the descriptions of observers and my own research, I found a "corporate America" that, in using college football game days to promote its various business enterprises, was "fast switching from the stadium box seat to the parking lot party." An American Tailgater marketing executive, speaking about this move from luxury skyboxes to luxury parking spots, put it most simply and eloquently: "It's more fun."[24]

The car, then, plays a large part in modern university life as corporate higher education continues to develop along edutainment lines. It is a third-place partner playing an important role in this development. It is the engine that moves the party from the stadium to the parking lot. The party in the parking lot has sauntered over from the vehicle's tailgate to the classrooms of the universities that issue the party invitations to their sports spectacles. Higher education, with the corporate push of edubusiness marketing and advanced technology, is well on the road to becoming edutainment. For parents preparing children for a higher education, and for their children-turned-university-students and their professors, the ride can be bumpy from start to finish.

THREE

Parents and Pedagogy

Helicopters and Expert Advice

Professionals are trained to give expert advice. Indeed, they understand advice-giving as an important occupational duty, a part of their special standing in the community they belong to. In this regard parents of university students receive more than their fair share of advice, heavily supplemented by the information-distributing capacity of the modern technology at use in today's version of "family."

Then too, parenting itself, with its fixed social-class differences, has over time become professionalized. Cultural analyst Christopher Lasch tells the story of how the factory system of the nineteenth century first socialized production away from the family unit and later led to the socialization of reproduction. As time passed child-rearing functions were gradually taken over by surrogate parents – "responsible not to the family but to the state, to private industry, or to their own codes of professional ethics." Lasch continues:

> In the course of bringing culture to the masses, the advertising industry, the mass media, the health and welfare services, and other agencies of mass tuition took over many of the socializing functions of the home and brought the ones that remained under the direction of modern science and technology. . . . [There developed] a consensus among the 'helping professions' that the family could no longer provide for its own needs. Doctors, psychiatrists, child development experts, spokesmen for the juvenile courts, marriage counselors, leaders of the public hygiene movement all said the same thing – usually reserving to their own professions, however, the leading role in the care of the young.[1]

Social class played a pivotal role in this transformation. Social reformers of all stripes, including social workers, feared class conflict and offered as remedy their conclusion that "outside agencies" had to make up for family deficiencies, as seen especially in the working-class family. In addition, the reformers gave voice to the idea that "the family promoted a narrow, parochial, selfish, and individualistic mentality and thus impeded the development of sociability and cooperation."[2]

As Lasch illustrates, in a matter of decades parents, under the duress of professional concern and criticism, came to doubt their fitness, or their abilities, to adequately parent their children. In the 1920s and 1930s professional educators and other helpers stepped in, armed with then-popular principles of behaviourist psychology that "stressed the need for strict feeding schedules and carefully regulated child-parent contacts." In the late 1930s and 1940s that behaviourism, with its overarching concern of freeing the child from an overly emotional attachment to parents, was replaced by a progressive permissiveness. The principle of feeding on demand replaced feeding schedules as the experts worried less about creating overly dependent children and urged parents to cater to the child's "needs." As Lasch puts it, "Love came to be regarded not as a danger but a positive duty."[3]

By the mid-1940s and into the 1950s expert wisdom had taken another turn. After its 1946 publication, Dr. Benjamin Spock's *Baby and Child Care* quickly became the child-rearing bible for parents of the "baby boom" generation and beyond.[4] Today, two and three generations later, it is still go-to reading material for new parents. Lasch contends that Spock, often mistakenly blamed for the excesses and failures of permissive child-rearing, "should be seen instead as one of its critics, seeking to restore the rights of the parent in the face of an exaggerated concern for the rights of the child."[5]

Telling critiques of both behaviourist and permissive child-rearing left a vacuum that led to a third stage in the development of expert advice. Lasch labels this new dogma "the cult of authenticity," which grew out of and alongside the various liberation movements of the late 1950s, 1960s, and early 1970s. The advice experts gave to parents was now to trust their own feelings – as long as these sentiments remained authentic and were conveyed spontaneously. Lasch summarizes:

> If the child expresses emotions that seem incommensurate with the occasion, the parent, instead of pointing out this discrepancy – instead of making an objective statement about reality and the emotions appropriate to it

– should indicate to the child that he understands the child's feelings and acknowledges his right to express them.

His conclusion: "The cult of authenticity reflects the collapse of parental guidance and provides it with a moral justification."[6] Expert advice was letting parents off the hook with regard to bearing significant responsibility for their children's behaviour.

This devaluation of parenthood was in turn quickly followed by movements in which parents attempted to wrest back control, to return to the family socialization functions long since relinquished and transferred over to expert wisdom and the accompanying institutions of factory and white-collar workplaces, schools, and government. This social control from outside the family eventually caused both parental dissatisfaction and anxiety and uncertainty for all concerned – which only served to feed the need for further expert advice from the professionals, who, as their wisdom was sought anew, could afford to remain somewhat aloof and unconcerned about the troubles resulting from past advice given. Parents and children alike internalized their acquiescence to, and some eager acceptance of, expert advice often disguised as social control. In his well-known study of the American high school, Edgar Z. Friedenberg repeatedly found that while students sometimes questioned authority, they generally regarded social control as "a technical problem, to be referred to the right expert for solution."[7] As Lasch notes, students and others can discredit and even participate in authority structures while leaving domination uncriticized and in place. Marxist theorists often talk about this as a matter of co-optation and alienation that reproduces the status quo.

Recent attempts to restore the family and parental rights lost over the past century have crossed several lines of social demarcation. A strong strategic theme has been to encourage parents to befriend their children, to become their pals if not necessarily their equals. This has resulted in what Neil Postman, among others, has recognized and labelled "the disappearance or end of childhood."[8] As adults try to keep up with the changing vocabularies, leisure-time pursuits, styles, and manners of their children, they themselves become more child-like; their children often attempt to meet them at least halfway by "hurrying" to become more adult-like.[9] In an era punctuated by rising rates of crime, delinquency, psychological breakdowns, and acts of violence, this phenomenon of child-like adults and adult-like children has been joined by a new mode of parental vigilance known as "helicopter parenting" –

when parents take an overprotective or excessive interest in the lives of their child or children.

The connections between professionalism, with its expert advice, and parenting have been fostered, aided and abetted, by the digital micro-technology developed over the past half-century. It is a technology that plays a significant role in parenting decisions and actions, often helping the so-called "helicopter parents" to hover over and monitor their children's behaviour. Critics of helicopter parenting argue that parental overprotection of children is not only unreasonably intrusive but often has harmful consequences. Career consultant Ashley Stahl speaks directly to helicopter parents about the several ways that their overzealous entry into the lives of their children may be forestalling and often completely preventing them from growing into responsible adults. For one thing, she says, "You're disempowering your child," which can result in a "struggle with problem-solving, low self-esteem and fear of failure." Helicopter kids have "higher levels of depression and anxiety," and, Stahl says, "Studies show that students with helicopter parents have a harder time finding employment after graduation."

The children will also lack "coping skills." Helicopter parenting "increases dependence and leads to diminished decision-making ability." The children won't have the "necessary skills to independently handle conflicts, disappointments, or failures." Instead, the parents are "equipping them with entitlement issues" and not allowing them "to know the feeling of true accomplishment."

As well, she tells the helicopter parents, "You're not even helping from an authentic place." Again, as she points out, "Studies show that this intrusive 'helicopter' behavior is driven by parental anxiety, rather than good intentions, as so many parents claim. . . . Roughly 25% of millennials say their parents are involved to the point of humiliation and annoyance."

Parents need to remember: "You're not going to live forever." And "Your kid will make less money" as an unwanted outcome of the low self-esteem that develops during adolescence. "Studies show that self-esteem is a positive indicator of future earnings."[10]

Stahl is not against close and loving parent-child relationships, but her argument rests on the understanding that "there is a world of difference between supporting your child and steering your child's life." She notes, "Millennials are now the most protected and programmed generation in history" – and this is so particularly in the area of job hunting and career moves. A third of the millennials reported that their parents were "very involved in their job hunt process." One in ten said their parents have accompanied them to job interviews, and a small number of "recent college graduates" had reported that their parents had "actually sat in on the interview." Some seven out of ten college recruits said they needed to speak to their parents before accepting a job offer.[11]

In another rapidly escalating trend, the colleges or universities themselves appear to be encouraging parents to become overinvolved in the admissions process. Hara Estroff Marano, an editor at *Psychology Today*, suggests that these institutions should know better:

> They are, after all, in the business of promoting the development of young adults. Instead, they see an opportunity for their own survival, and some are going so far as to actually cultivate parental invasiveness. So many parents now show up for campus visits on admitted-student days that the University of Texas law school in Austin has quadrupled the number of such days it holds. An administrator at another graduate school advises that parents be looked on not as overzealous but as trusted partners and "benefactors," and that wooing parents can be the pipeline to more applicants.[12]

The critiques of Marano and Stahl are not lone voices on the helicopter-ing front, and some analysts strive to debunk what they see as the myth of the helicopter parent. Education and parenting writer Alfie Kohn describes "the pernicious cultural biases" behind what he sees as "a collegiate urban legend." Going beyond anecdotal evidence, he examines hard data indicating that while most parents do indeed keep in touch with their college-age kids on a regular basis, "Communicating isn't the same thing as intervening on a child's behalf, and the latter seems to be fairly rare."[13]

Kohn cites 2009 U.S. research, the National Survey of Student Engagement (NSSE), which found that among the 900 students at 24 colleges and universities only 13 per cent of college first-year students and 8 per cent of seniors said "a parent had frequently intervened to help them solve problems." In another 2009 study, this time of more than 10,000 University of California students, the majority reported that "their parents weren't involved in their choice of courses or their major." In a third study, Michigan State University researchers found that 77 per cent of 725 employers surveyed "hardly ever witnessed a parent while hiring a college senior." Other studies suggest that helicoptering seems to apply to no more than 20 per cent of parent-child relationships.

Furthermore, and most important in backing Kohn's view, some studies show that frequent parental involvement and support of all kinds contributed to the well-being of young adults. The NSSE study, for example, directly contradicted the notion of deleterious educational consequences being traceable to helicopter parenting: "Compared with their counterparts, children of helicopter parents were more satisfied with every aspect of their college experience, gained more in such areas as writing and critical thinking, and were more likely to talk with faculty and peers about substantive topics."[14]

Satisfying school experiences are, of course, just one instance that reveals the importance of understanding parent-child relations within a larger social context. Kohn's review and the other helicopter discussions suggest the critical role played by what sociologists refer to as variations in "cultural capital,"[15] as these intersect with differences in social class, gender, and ethnicity. Rather than angrily blaming either parents and/or children in the helicopter scenario, a better road to understanding this phenomenon in its cultural context is to take subtle but clear distinctions into account. Kohn, for example, reminds us that "independence" (and the importance of fostering it) "is closely connected to an individualistic worldview that is far from universal," with other cultures and classes being "more likely to emphasize the value of interdependence." As he notes, a useful distinction may be to recognize that "maturity isn't the same as [individualistic] self-sufficiency."[16] A careful analysis of cultural context, then – including the pivotal role played by social class as well as technology and architectural changes in our built environment – is fundamental to our understanding of why parents might become overinvolved in the lives of their children.

In 2014 a working mom in South Carolina became the focus of heated discussion when she was taken into police custody for permitting her nine-year-old daughter to go to the park alone. This incident not only raised the expected safety and security issues but also initiated an emotionally charged debate over how much latitude parents should have in bringing up their children.[17] The debate has underlined the importance of social-class differences that influence parenting in relation to when, under what circumstances, and how forcefully the state should be allowed to enter the realm of *in loco parentis*.

Parents of the middle, upper-middle, professional, and upper classes often accompany their children to park playgrounds. The play areas are designed so that the playground equipment is located at a central point, with benches and tables arranged in a circle close by. Here parents can engage in conversation while at the same time they are able – and this is key – to keep a watchful protective eye as their children interact with others. As Holly Blackford, among others, notes, this playground architecture bears a striking resemblance to the panopticon of the prison as described and analyzed by French social analyst Michel Foucault in his well-known writings on discipline and punishment.[18] The arrangement is well suited to helicopter parents, both encouraging and reinforcing them in their desire to monitor their children closely.

The children of parents from the working- and underclasses, though, often must make do with the indoor playgrounds provided by fast-food eateries such as McDonald's and Burger King. These indoor play areas are constructed in such a way that the parental view or gaze is often blocked, making it difficult, if not impossible, for parents to observe and monitor what is going on among their children. Helicopter parenting is severely curtailed by this physical structure, and both parents and children may grow accustomed to, maybe even prefer, this way of ordering their worlds. McDonald's children at play are routinely left to their own devices with neither the benefits nor the drawbacks of the parental oversight and interference provided to the helicoptered kids of Foucault's octagon. These differences in how play is structured and patterned constitute part of a larger cultural context; and they reveal the importance of social class in our thinking about childhood and when and how this period in the life cycle comes to an end.

As Postman, in his concern over the disappearance of childhood, makes clear: the opportunities for children to be childlike during a certain period of their lives are accompanied by, and run alongside of, developments in technology. Much of his analysis was echoed in two other books from the early 1980s: Valerie Polakow Suransky, *The Erosion of Childhood*, and Marie Winn, *Children Without Childhood*. A central theme for all three authors, in addition to charting significant changes in the school and the family as basic societal institutions, is the increasingly large role played by technology in our "electronic age."

Postman's focus is the impact of the media of communication on the socialization of children. He argues that the printing press created childhood and that the electronic media, starting with television, are now "disappearing" it. He shows how Gutenberg's invention created and encouraged a strong connection between print literacy and adulthood, with children being those who have yet to earn this adult status by

mastering the art of reading. For Postman, then, twentieth-century electronic media were fast destroying the print culture equation that formerly connected literacy, schools, and the separation of childhood from
adulthood. He is especially convincing when analyzing the impact of
television, "the total disclosure medium,"[19] and how it encourages
adults to be more like children and encourages children to disappear, to
become increasingly similar to the evermore childlike adults.

Polakow's work draws upon data collected from eight preschool
centres located in and around Chicago. Her participant-observation
approach provides a picture of what goes on in the everyday world of
children's daycare as the kids interact in work-play away from the television. Observed class and gender differences are important in the distinction she draws between "lived-time" and "institutional time." Her
discussion urging the deinstitutionalization of childhood is based on a
premise supported by the study's data that "the being of childhood is
thus seen to be antithetical to the life of the institution."[20]

Winn's analysis complements Polakow's in that she too focuses her
concern on the school and even more particularly and directly upon the
changing family relationships between mothers and their children. Her
data from "hundreds of interviews" with both children and parents indicates that modern parenting, in contrast to earlier times, requires a
much more collaborative relationship. This more democratic and less
authoritarian style, supported by the expert advice of professionals,
leaves both parents and their kids confused and uncertain as to what is
expected regarding the roles they are to play. Typical of this confusion,
which brings Postman's "adult-child" and "disappearing child" back full
circle, is a response from one of Winn's interviewees, a thirteen-year-old
eighth-grader from upstate New York:

> It's sort of weird, but my mother is like my age sometimes. She's discover-
> ing things about life at the same time I am, having boyfriends, and having
> men sleep over. She even asks me questions about sex. This is very confus-
> ing for her, and makes me very confused too a lot of the time. And some-
> times she's very strict, but then she's also very loose about things.[21]

Winn echoes Postman's concern with the developing technology of electronic media when she turns to the topic of children's play in her chapter
"The End of Play." She emphasizes significant changes in the games that
children play – video games versus marbles, for example – and the
impact of the mere presence of television in altering traditional parent-
child relationships. In her thesis, similar to Postman's, she follows the

thinking of communication studies pioneers Harold Innis and Marshall McLuhan: that what is most important is not the programming content of what children watch but, rather, the structure of the television medium itself.[22] To repeat McLuhan's well-known aphorism, the medium is both the message and the massage. Each new medium we experience has a form or mould, the structural boundaries and limitations of which we more or less unconsciously incorporate. In this manner form becomes content that changes us in ways we often do not perceive. Educational theorists refer to these undetected effects of form as school's "hidden curriculum." This idea has been expressed by stressing the importance of how one is taught rather than what one is taught, encouraging many school observers and reformers to focus on reorganizing school structure and on learning process rather than products or outcomes.

In an earlier book, *The Plug-In Drug*, Winn speaks to the hidden curriculum of out-of-control television viewing – its debilitating effect on what should be the spontaneity and magical playfulness of childhood:

> Only with the fascinating presence of television in every home, mesmerizing and sedating normally unpredictable and demanding children, was the actual decrease in adult attention and supervision made possible. This conjunction occurred in the 1960s. Suddenly the idea of childhood as a special and protected condition came to seem inadvisable if not actually dangerous, and in any event, quite impossible to maintain.[23]

These observations about television remind us that media technology in its application is not simply a neutral conveyor of information. Each new communications "advancement," such as internet technology reliant upon computer, cellphone, tablet, and various social media platforms, changes and reorganizes the structure of our interests and interactions.

Technology, Parenting Styles, and Questions of Culture

The prevailing changes and reorganization are emphasized in a 2015 newspaper feature on how electronic technology alters family relationships. Journalist Dave McGinn's article "Parents, It's Not Just the Kids Who Need to Step away from the Screens" carries a warning for the oldsters about how they need to disconnect from their electronic devices. McGinn cites a survey of more than 6,000 parents and children (between the ages of eight and thirteen) across nine countries, including Canada, conducted by online security company AVG Technologies. The company found that "54 per cent of kids felt parents checked their devices too often. And 36 per cent said their biggest grievance was when parents became distracted by their device during conversation, which made 32 per cent of kids feel unimportant." In elaborating, McGinn borrows from work done by clinical psychologist and author Catherine Steiner-Adair, whose work speaks to the potential damaging emotional and psychological consequences of parents' addiction to screens. Her interviews of kids ranging in age from four to eighteen reveal that often the youngsters are playing second fiddle to their parents' technology, resulting in feelings of loneliness, anger, and frustration. She cites as typical what "a lot of kids said, 'I must just be boring to my dad because when we're together he's texting.' . . . They feel like they just don't matter enough."

In thinking about what happens when kids feel they don't matter enough, McGinn draws upon the work of pediatrician Jenny Radesky and her colleagues at Boston Medical Center. They observed fifty-five groups of parents and children at fast-food restaurants. McGinn reports, "A majority of adults – 40 of them – took out a mobile device during the meal." Perhaps the statistics of this observation do not offer anything especially concerning. But the researchers observed a "disconcerting pattern": "The more parents were absorbed by devices, the more likely their children were to act out. The kids' misbehaviour was likely an attempt to get their parents' attention."[24]

Parental inattention fuelled by technology results in device-neglected kids who act out in a manner that forces parents to pay closer attention, at least in the moment. This whirligig of demonstrated inattention and forced attention reclaimed imposes a pattern of interaction on both parties, adults and children. Although its genesis is different, parental screen neglect reminds us of, and returns us to, the issue of helicopter parents. In both cases the need to parent with renewed vigour becomes paramount as the interaction circle closes in on the inevitable repetition, the next reiteration, of the pattern. In both cases the role of technology is centre stage and increasingly important. Television ads celebrate the wonders of technology in a manner that encourages helicopter parents, whether they are caught up in screen culture or not, to continue their hovering and expand it. One such ad touts the latest technology's merits, useful not only for correcting parental oversight in forgetting to close the garage door but extending parental reach, allowing parents at work to check on the whereabouts of their kids and to monitor what they are doing (homework?) and who they are hanging out with (which friends came home from school with them?). Seemingly, with the coming-of-age of drone technology, this monitoring from afar will become easier and more complete.

The melding of innovative technology and today's parenting styles carries important consequences. Hovering parents, and maybe even screen-culture-addicted ones who are failing in face-to-face interaction, are no doubt implicated in what Greg Lukianoff and Jonathan Haidt see as "The Coddling of the American Mind." College coddling is repre-sented by two terms that "have risen quickly from obscurity into com-mon campus parlance": "microaggressions" and "trigger warnings." The aggressions are "small actions or word choices that seem on their face to have no malicious intent but that are thought of as a kind of violence nonetheless." By way of example the authors note that some campus guidelines suggest that asking an Asian American or Latino American "Where were you born?" can be offensive because such a question could be interpreted as implying that the person being addressed is not a "real American." The other term, trigger warnings, refers to "alerts that pro-fessors are expected to issue if something in a course might cause a strong emotional response." For example, some students have targeted F. Scott Fitzgerald's novel *The Great Gatsby* as problematic in its portrayal of misogyny and physical abuse and want warnings to be issued to pro-tect potential readers who have previously been victimized by domestic violence.[25]

For Lukianoff and Haidt this protective concern has created a "new climate [that] is slowly being institutionalized, and is affecting what can be said in the classroom, even as a basis for discussion." For some observ-ers these developments are seen as a re-emergence of the so-called "politi-cal correctness" movement of the 1990s, but the authors see a significant difference between then and now. The political correctness movement "sought to restrict speech (specifically hate speech aimed at marginalized groups), but it also challenged the literary, philosophical, and historical canon, seeking to widen it by including more diverse perspectives." In contrast, the new movement is essentially about "emotional well-being . . . it presumes an extraordinary fragility of the collegiate psyche, and therefore elevates the goal of protecting students from psychological harm," thereby turning "campuses into 'safe spaces' where young adults are shielded from words and ideas that make some uncomfortable."[26]

We are on tricky educational ground here, as the authors point out in elaborating their argument. Teaching students to develop a questioning mind and critical thinking skills in this protection-first environment is becoming ever more challenging because "such questioning often leads to discomfort, and even to anger, on the way to understanding." Essentially the new university environment encourages "claims of a right not to be offended." Lukianoff and Haidt explain: "Everyone is supposed to rely upon his or her own subjective feelings to decide whether a comment by a professor or a fellow student is unwelcome, and therefore grounds for a harassment claim. Emotional reasoning is now accepted as evidence."[27] In my view, a higher education of value should call upon the emotions – but the emotional burden of this new university environment poses significant dangers to scholarship. Professors pull the plug on some important course-related readings, making them optional, and censor relevant topics that might have otherwise been the focus of class discussions, speeding up the creation of a staid, predictable, and protected learning environment devoid of spontaneity and humour. Professors are joined by students as they manoeuvre through an increasingly complicated academic maze with the fear of possible administrative reprisals and lawsuits guiding their lessons. Perhaps even the discussion on these pages, with its concern over class and privilege differences, might be viewed by students as unwelcome writing that makes them feel uncomfortable. Perhaps I had better make this reading optional in future courses I teach. It is easy to see how a climate marked by a kind of "vindictive protectiveness" can be viewed in its cultural context as the institutional equivalent to the worst aspects of helicopter parenting.

Lukianoff and Haidt are clear that the new university environment is of no benefit to most students. They argue that "the increased focus on microaggressions coupled with the endorsement of emotional reasoning is a formula for a constant state of outrage, even toward well-meaning speakers trying to engage in genuine discussion." They ask: "What are we doing to our students if we encourage them to develop extra-thin skin just before they leave the cocoon of adult protection and enter the workforce?" They answer with another question: "Would they not be better prepared to flourish if we taught them to question their own emotional reactions, and to give people the benefit of the doubt?" Joining these deliberations surrounding today's overly protective university environment with our discussion of helicopter parenting, we arrive at the same caution: college students might well benefit from less protection, and it would be better for them to learn how to handle mental associations that cause them discomfort, "because the world beyond college will be far less willing to accommodate requests for trigger warnings and opt-outs."[28]

None of this is to say that there will not be cases that warrant trigger warnings, and some students should be given options to pass on/withdraw from classroom presentations and material that may cause severe emotional trauma (rape, domestic violence, child abuse, and the trauma that continues to haunt First Nations residential school survivors and their families are examples). Also, none of this is to say that discriminating actions based upon prejudicial beliefs should be tolerated. On the contrary, sexism, racism, classism, homophobia, and the like should be called out, denounced, and actively discouraged both inside and outside the confines of the campus. Rather, it is to say that today's higher education, at times pathologically concerned with protection and too often permeated with accompanying fearfulness, is creating a particular kind of learning environment. It is an educational context too often detrimental to the free expression of ideas, as well as to the differing interpretations and debates that routinely arise as the result of free exchanges – and, more generally, detrimental with regard to the creativity that marks scholarship at its best. As Lukianoff and Haidt recognize, this new university environment is not "political correctness" coming back in disguise, old wine in new bottles. Rather, in its connection to helicopter parenting and larger concerns over prevailing ideas about childhood, everyday routine in U.S. and Canadian universities today is as much about what constitutes the appropriate role for both parents and schools to play, and how to foster effective connections between them, than it is about anything else.

American anthropologist David Lancy, having done extensive fieldwork in Papua New Guinea and Liberia, with more limited time spent in Madagascar, Uganda, Trinidad, and Sweden, has studied these matters and formed some definite opinions, often controversial, about how we raise children in our society. Lancy labels Western countries as "neontocracies" – societies in which children are seen as the most valued members. He notes that neontocracy grows up alongside, or accompanies, economic development. Summarizing his forty-some years of fieldwork comparing other societies and cultures in developing nations with our own, he points out: "Western, middle-class parents are much too worried about protecting children from perceived threats and optimizing their development. They believe there is one right way to raise children, and even a slight deviation from it causes measurable harm. My review of child-rearing patterns elsewhere shows that it is impossible to identify one best or 'normal' practice."[29]

Lancy also reminds us that historically the great majority of societies have been gerontocracies, where elders have been the most valued members – which leads him to a second point connecting childhood to school: "Actually for most of human history there was no such thing as childhood. Children were viewed as small, incompetent adults. It wasn't until the Victorian era that people began to see children as occupying a distinct stage in human development, with different needs, vulnerabilities, and understandings. This eventually led to the abolition of child labor and the rise of formal schooling."[30] In brief, our culture and this moment in time both occupy "outlier" status. They come together as an "abnormality" both cross-culturally and across the historical timeline.

This constant emphasis upon overprotecting children from the moment of their birth is carried on in our system of formal schooling, from kindergarten right through graduate school. Whether it is parents arranging and scripting "playdates" for their young children, or those same children turned into university students who later find themselves forced to rely on their professors to direct them in their scholarly activities, young people in our society are protected from making choices and mistakes that are at the heart of learning how to be in the adult world. To borrow physicist and Ph.D. graduate Jeff Schmidt's delightful phrase used to describe how graduate school experience shapes the lives of salaried professionals in making subject matter and project choices on the road to graduation and research funding, both students and faculty learn "assignable curiosity and ideology."[31]

In discussing this family-school nexus of overprotection and its learning drawbacks and shortcomings, Lancy speculates on what might result if parents in developing countries modelled themselves after their American (or Canadian) counterparts: "If parents were to play a more active and protective role in their child's development, the children might be safer from injury, but that sense of autonomy and ability to learn independently would be undermined. The children would cease to take the initiative to learn new things and instead wait for an adult's permission, guidance, or instruction."[32] Assignable curiosity indeed.

Lancy considers the virtues of what he calls the "chore curriculum," a reference to children gaining knowledge of their culture by mastering chores. "It isn't top-down and formal [like our schools] but rather emerges from a child's desire to fit in and emulate older siblings and relatives." For me, this socialization through chores bears some resemblance to our apprenticeship programs, which some schools have been moved to resurrect after years of neglect and disinterest. As Lancy notes, this kind of learning through observation and doing is made easier in a village, an environment in which "the technology is visible and accessible," with "a low bar to getting involved in most activities." Children learn early on how to travel relatively long distances from home to gather water and to forage for food and fire-making material. He is "struck by how strange schooling looks from an anthropological perspective. So much about formal education is antithetical to the way children have learned throughout history. Jump to the twenty-first century, and a childhood without schooling is unthinkable."[33]

For Lancy, then, "Parenting trends are less about what's good for the child and more about parents' need for affirmation." He states that the message of his work is that "parents have far less impact than they think they do."[34] While agreeing, I would add that the impact they do have is often deleterious and causes harm in the ways he describes. As with overprotective parenting, our overreliance on school as the one best way to educate, as the foundation of learning, and on advanced technology as an increasingly desirable mediator of learning means that the price of participation can be dangerously high, even unhealthy.

A 2016 *Toronto Star* headline declared, "Internet takes a bite out of food budget." The story related how "low-income Canadians are taking money out of their budgets for food, recreation and rent to pay for Internet service," with a new report indicating that "the high costs of obtaining high-speed home Internet connections can lead to unnecessary hardship."[35] To overcome this barrier to civic participation an advocacy group was urging the Canadian government to mandate lower connection fees for low-income families and individuals. For many reasons – opportunities for employment, access to government services, and whatever sociability and learning benefits social media may provide – I support such an initiative.

Further down on the same page an article described a new campaign pushing for increasing Indigenous participation in higher education. The Council of Ontario Universities (COU) was taking part in hopes of significantly adding to the 6,500 Aboriginal students enrolled in Ontario's universities – "only 9 per cent of Ontario aboriginal residents have a university degree, compared with 23 percent of non-aboriginal people." The article cited a lack of role models as a "key barrier" to increasing Aboriginal participation in post-secondary education.[36]

The lack-of-role-models argument is certainly credible and no doubt true. It is, though, a problem that could in large part be solved simply by making future decisions that would privilege and feature First Nations traditional cultural practices and experiences in our educational institutions. This initiative would significantly change curricula and standard classroom protocol and would result in the creation of Indigenous role models in our colleges and universities. Such changes might also be useful in toning down and overcoming our unhealthy fixation on technology and the implementation of high-tech e-learning as the necessary and sufficient fix for higher learning.

In the end the new climate of overprotection found in today's college and university settings is tightly linked both to the institutional structures that train and educate advice-giving experts and to the ubiquitous advice-giving experts who permeate everyday life on all fronts – all of which only adds encouragement to the debilitating polite civility and servility of the professionalism that surrounds us all.

FOUR

Professionals and Professionalism

Protecting the Status Quo and Academic Disciplines

Autonomy plus commitment and responsibility – those terms characterize the professional occupational environment, at least insomuch as those conditions can be narrowly applied to a specific workplace or discipline. It is an environment that is also characterized by civility and servility – and the presence of civility complements and encourages yet another characteristic, often described as the authority of colleagues. That feature refers to the network of interactions and relationships that oversees entry into and maintenance of favourable standing within the profession. Practitioners within the vertically structured social context of service to the hierarchical relations of bureaucracy often maintain their own professional boundaries, policed by the horizontal authority of credentialed colleagues.

The dictum that warns employees not to question bureaucratic authority coalesces with a certain coddling of minds. At first glance this may seem a rather odd pairing, but the combination is routinely on display in today's universities. Exemplary and instructive is the 2015 case of Dr. Alexander Coward, a lecturer in mathematics at the University of California at Berkeley. When Coward was threatened with losing his non-tenure-track job despite six years of stellar student reviews, his students objected with a show of force. Nearly three thousand of them came to his defence by signing a petition, and some fifty of his most ardent supporters attended a protest held on October 20, the day the university set to formally review its decision not to renew his contract.

Coward's teaching philosophy centres on the question of how to motivate students to work hard. In a December 2014 letter sent to his department chair, Coward acknowledged that tangible rewards such as better grades for better work are one option, but went on to cite considerable research stressing the benefits of "intrinsic motivation." He said that encouraging the "motivation that's bubbling up inside ourselves because we're curious and like to learn and like to improve is much more powerful than saying, 'I'm going to do this because it's 0.7777 of my GPA [grade point average].'"[1]

Accordingly, Coward tries to foster a feeling of "autonomy, competency, and personal affinity" rather than relying on "humdrum grades" to motivate students. In his classes he repeatedly asks if the students understand the concepts being taught and offers numerous repetitions and insightful variations of explanations. Students report that he always makes time for them when they need help. While he chooses not to administer standard customary measures of progress, such as graded homework and quizzes, he does provide the traditional end-of-course final examinations and marks required by the school bureaucracy.

Coward's teaching philosophy and style seem to work. His students go on to succeed in more advanced math courses, and year after year he receives higher evaluations than those given to other department faculty – higher than any of the regular faculty teaching the Introductory Math 1A course. Yet the math department still found enough problems with his approach to question his suitability as a teacher. In a 2013 email to Coward, Arthur Angus, a former chair of the department, delivered a veiled warning designed to get the wayward lecturer to knuckle under. "I do think it [sic] that it is very important that you not deviate too far from the department norms." This sentiment was repeated several times in subsequent emails and memos. As Coward responded in a blog post: "This raises the question, What does it mean to adhere to department norms if one has the highest student evaluation scores in the department, students performing statistically significantly better in subsequent courses and faculty observations universally reporting 'extraordinary skills at lecturing, presentation and engaging students'?" His answer: "In a nutshell: stop making us look bad. If you don't, we'll fire you."

In the end Coward decided he could not follow the department's professional bureaucratic script because it would mean abandoning his teaching principles and philosophy: "I absolutely love teaching the students at Berkeley, but I cannot in good conscience follow the instructions you have given me. I am unwilling to go to work and feel ashamed of what I am doing any more."

The Coward case represents and illustrates the coming together, the joining, of two types of authority: the professional authority of colleagues and the hierarchical authority of bureaucratic office. Even if they receive glowing reviews and indications of superior student performance, the undergraduate students occupying the lowest rung on the academic hierarchy are seen as non-professionals who need further training to ensure that they follow the judgments and decisions of their betters. This thinking and these outcomes are repeated daily on college and university campuses across North America. The typical academic tone of civility was apparent in the deliberations, charges, and rebuttals at Berkeley (although Coward did charge the math department and university administrators with "bullying"). Also clearly in evidence was a demand for servility. Together, the role of servility and civility in reproducing status quo arrangements brings to mind the now legendary student protests of the 1960s and the part played by professionals and professionalism in keeping the lid on campus unrest.

The popular press, as I've reflected elsewhere, continues to sum up the ten years between 1963 and 1973 "with the now infamous phrase *sex, drugs, and rock 'n' roll*." But beyond free love, pot and acid, Woodstock, love-ins, and flower power were the serious on-campus political movements of free speech, Black power, women's liberation, and Students for a Democratic Society (SDS). All of this, if not initiated by college and university students, found strong campus support among them as they organized and participated in marches, rallies, and campus teach-ins during the height of the Vietnam conflict. And this was a "global phenomenon," as the 1968 student protest movements also sprang up in the United Kingdom, France, Germany (East and West), Spain, the Scandinavian countries, Yugoslavia, Czechoslovakia, Hungary, and Poland. Protests pounded those in power in Mexico, Argentina, and Brazil. Throughout this period – again reflecting the poverty of professionalism:

> The driving force behind the anti-war movement was the students and not their professors. American students were joined by their counterparts around the world in an increasingly global resistance to doing 'business as usual' while most of their faculty instructors and international colleagues were busy propping up and protecting the status quo against prodemocracy movements that might lead to fundamental social change.[2]

Professionalism, Professional Associations, and the Status Quo: The Demands of Civility and Servility

The professional norms and practices that have governed the daily behaviour of scholars over the decades – and notably the reaffirmation of status quo economic arrangements – are starkly illustrated by events at two 1968 annual meetings: that of the American Sociological Association (ASA) and the American Political Science Association (APSA). In his "view from below" of the ASA meetings, Martin Nicolaus points out that as early as 1960–61 the ASA was receiving 80 per cent of its budget from the corporation and government contracts that it was "servicing." This cozy arrangement, Nicolaus says, produces a servility that features an "official" sociology, endorsed by the ASA, that links the United States via military and indoctrination campaigns to foreign hotspots worldwide. These global ties help to ensure what he refers to as a "pledge of allegiance" type of socialization at home via formal education in elementary and high schools, colleges, and universities. In this scenario a significant segment of sociology B.A.s find employment in "official," often public, bureaucracies; career success and handsome rewards clearly accrue to those willing to reaffirm and therefore renew the servility cycle as depicted by Nicolaus.[3]

He argues that the ASA sells an "official view of the social scene" to a non-professional public, while at the same time continuing to exercise control over professional colleagues. This reality is made possible by the organization's formal political – and elitist – mechanisms, which permit the continuation of a caste system in which the upper caste ("composed of full-time responsible Ph.D.'d professional sociologists employed by universities, business, or government") elects the president, vice-president, and a twelve-member Council whose power is "beyond appeal."[4] Such an undemocratic organizational set-up helps keep sensitive matters in-house, because after all professional sociologists and other social scientists for hire must not only be civil and servile but also discreet in their dealings. Those involved in the Michigan State–CIA sponsored Vietnam Project and Project Camelot of the 1960s discovered this to be the case when embarrassing operational and financial details of their work were made public by outsiders not interested in playing by the rules of their professional game.

A 1969 review of political scientists and the routine practices of the APSA by Alan Wolfe provides a companion piece to Nicolaus's analysis of the undemocratic elitist practices of the ASA. Wolfe argues that in structuring their own professional association these scholars of politics have

been unable to put into practice the pluralism they preach. He emphasizes the unrepresentative character of the association's business meetings, nominating committee, and elections as evidence. All this fits well,
he notes, with the then-new conservatism taught by many university
professors, an ideology steeped in anti-participatory and conservative
optimism. Leading theorists Daniel Bell and Seymour M. Lipset espouse
that optimism, with Bell issuing a declaration that ideology is dead and
Lipset declaring that any debate, if still necessary, should take its lead
from the premise that "the fundamental political problems of the industrial revolution have been solved."[5] As Wolfe points out, professional
political scientists of the time were not against reform. Their approach
was much more subtle, acknowledging the need for certain reforms
while attempting to ensure that the purpose of change was to *conserve*
the established structures.[6] This type of gradualism – which, while
appearing to be somewhat progressive, protects the status quo – has
long characterized reforms advocated by American sociologists.[7] Reform
that might lead to fundamental social change, then, has never played a
major role and is not a top priority in the activities of professional associations; rather, their focus is on social control.

The Many Faces of Social Control

Professional organizations exercise control over their members in many
ways, including efforts to socialize the professionals to learn how to
police themselves. Publication outlets are an important control mechanism, accompanied by peer reviewers' determination of the content
deemed suitable for publication.

As of 2016, the American Sociological Association was publishing ten
journals: *American Sociological Review, Contemporary Sociology, Contexts,
Journal of Health and Social Behavior, Social Psychological Quarterly,
Sociological Methodology, Sociological Theory, Sociology of Education,
Socius,* and *Teaching Sociology.* The ASA also has four "section journals":
City and Community (Section on Community and Urban Sociology), *Jour-
nal of World Systems Research* (Section on Political Economy of the World
System), *Sociology and Mental Health* (Section on Sociology of Mental
Health), and *Sociology of Race and Ethnicity* (Section for Racial and Ethnic
Minorities).[8]

This imposing list surely aims to be all-encompassing in its influence.
It is buttressed by the monographs in the ASA Rose Series in Sociology,

established in 1967 through a bequest to the ASA from sociologists Arnold and Caroline Rose. The Series Mission statement makes a bow to senior scholars – those who have already proved themselves inside the highly bureaucratized professional and university hierarchies – and adheres closely to the in-house thinking of professionals and their communities of interaction. Its first paragraph states:

> The ASA Rose Series in Sociology publishes highly visible, accessible books that integrate specific substantive areas in sociology. The books are designed to offer synthetic analyses of these fields, challenging prevailing paradigms, and/or offer fresh views of enduring controversies. *The authors are typically senior scholars who work with and review the best available evidence*, and utilize this evidential foundation to develop and defend their analysis. In most cases the arguments are extended to address contemporary public issues, and therefore reflect on or contribute to public policy. Because of their broad scope and policy relevance, *the volumes published in the Rose Series are disseminated in areas beyond their focus to the broader professional and intellectual communities*.[9]

A second paragraph pays particular attention to the role of qualified professionals and an editing process that the ASA describes as "the most thorough editing available in academic book publishing." The initial book proposal and changes in the book's construction are reviewed by seven series editors. "A mid-course review (scheduled once drafts of the core of the book are complete) includes careful reading by at least two editors, *a public colloquium* on the book's content *before a qualified professional audience*, and a detailed one-day critical discussion with the editors." After that, "The final draft is sent to *two top scholars who are lavishly rewarded* for a detailed, lengthy and timely review."[10]

The tight in-house control exercised by the ASA over this series ensures the continued hegemony of the professionals socialized and promoted within the discipline of sociology. In her 1967 path-breaking examination of the gatekeepers of science, Diana Crane emphasizes how this peer review controls and connects in an interlocking manner the communication channels of scientific research and publication.[11] As of 2014 the ASA with its Rose Series had published a total of 79 books. The first 13, from 1971 through 1975, were published under the auspices of the ASA itself. For the next 35, 1977–92, the ASA used Cambridge University Press, and after that, for the next 11, 1993–95, Rutgers University Press. With the turn of the century the ASA finally left the cozy confines of university presses behind, and the last 20 books in the series, from 2001 through 2013, were collaboratively published bearing the imprint of the Russell Sage Foundation (RSF).

One of the oldest U.S. foundations, RSF was established – for "the improvement of social and living conditions in the United States" – in 1907 with a $10-million gift from philanthropist Margaret Olivia Sage, the widowed beneficiary of wealthy Wall Street financier and railroad executive Russell Sage. The foundation's emphasis on social issues was clearly evident from the beginning as it "undertook major projects in low-income housing, urban planning, social work, and labor reform." Thereafter the RSF showed a change in emphasis from direct intervention to an academic focus on research and policy-making. "The foundation now dedicates itself exclusively to strengthening the methods, data, and theoretical core of the social sciences as a means of diagnosing social problems and improving social policies." Its list of visiting scholar, research, and book publishing programs invites collaborations with "other foundations, granting agencies and academic institutions in studies of social problems."[12] In a sentence with a Lincolnesque twist, the RSF is said to be a home of, by, and for academic professionals. Its adherents are, by and large, not interested in getting their hands dirty or in doing much thinking about how to fundamentally change prevailing arrangements.

The foundation's academic emphasis on controlled social reform that serves to reproduce the status quo was clearly outlined a half-century ago. In a 1967 research report on the RSF, Jay Schulman, Carol Brown, and Roger Kahn focused on the foundation in order to study "some of the ways in which sociology, sociologists, and collectivities of sociologists and social scientists foster elite domination in the United States by pursuing professional interests and projecting professional ideologies which reflect a mobile upper-middle class situation."[13] As I put it some years ago in a review of their work: "The authors find upper-middle-class professors, as a group, are linked to a few powerful individuals, a power elite, because they share a belief that individual achievement is recognized and rewarded, that social control is more requisite for the general welfare than is social change, and that beneficial social change can only be brought about through the action of 'authorities.'"[14] The RSF and other foundations – like the professors whose research they sponsor – routinely "appear before the public" as the organizations of the "disinterested scholar," but in actuality they serve to legitimate the authority of "authorities."[15]

Schulman, Brown, and Kahn argue that the foundation's dissemination and communication practices foster and reinforce this attitude of scholarly objectivity and autonomy. These writers' review of which persons and organizations get complementary copies of foundation-sponsored books and a more lengthy routine-announcements list leads to their working hypothesis regarding RSF's view of knowledge as power: "It need merely to be produced and published to have a beneficial effect."[16] Not only does academic professionalism find a welcoming home at RSF through the foundation's communication links with the top echelons of the knowledge industry both within and outside of universities, but these same links also provide a network that protects both foundation-academic civility and respectful servility from unwanted intrusions by the recipients of the decisions of "authorities" at the bottom of the social-class structure.[17] This "managerial sociology" focuses on identifying and helping to solve social problems in a way that leaves the status quo unchanged while protecting the entitlements and professional standing of all the helpers, academic sociologists included. In the words of the authors: "Frequently it appears that members of the knowledge industry are simultaneously the generators, producers, the packagers, distributors and consumers of their own product. The only thing they are not is their own funding source, a situation that they and the Russell Sage Foundation appear intent on remedying."[18]

A 1968 book by Christopher Jencks and David Riesman, *The Academic Revolution*, amplifies this discussion of peer-reviewed content deemed suitable for publication. Jencks, then a youthful up-and-comer beginning to make a name for himself in sociological circles, and Riesman, a well-published and widely acknowledged writer honoured as one of the leading scholars in the discipline, argued that the intellectual veto power of professional educators gave them control in shaping a higher education that is autonomous – so much so that the university, under the direction of the increasingly powerful professors, was fast becoming the dominant institution of the American social system. Riesman's blinders on this overstatement might be somewhat forgiven, perhaps attributable in part to his role as top advisor for the ACE (American Council on Education) – a board of well-known professional educators who in effect formed a government lobby for the education industry. He and Jencks explained university dominance by arguing that professional fitness for service in this leadership position came about as a result of intensive training in one of the academic disciplines, those groups they label "the racecourses of the mind."[19] According to Jencks and Riesman, future educators taking their positions on one of these racecourses and jockeying for position necessarily began to objectively separate their professional from their personal lives. The newly socialized professors come to believe not only that the universities containing the racecourses are autonomous, but also that, as professional scientists, they too can act autonomously (professionally). They learn to make few attempts at gaining genuine respect for their expertise from those outside of "the profession" and lower down in the status hierarchy. Instead, as professionals they learn to devalue and ignore the wishes, needs, and knowledge of "clients" in order to gain the approval of colleagues.

The Jencks-Riesman argument, then, combines their education-as-autonomous thesis with a narrow scientistic professionalism that is not only mutually reinforcing but also beneficial to a powerful socio-economic elite interested in maintaining their Wall Street and Bay Street perch atop the current economy. It is an argument that goes a long way towards ensuring that everyone, professional and non-professional alike, knows their assigned place and remains in it. Their colleague-oriented view of academic professionalism protects the elite academic schools – Harvard and Yale and a select few others outside the Ivy League, and their prestigious alumni – against an influx of too many clients-turned-colleagues from "the wrong side of the tracks." Or, to remain within the Jencks-Riesman metaphor, the institutions' view of the racecourses they were instrumental in designing did not allow for much "off-track betting." Later, in another book, *Inequality*, Jencks would argue that decisions as to who is permitted to run the racecourses, like the benefits that might possibly obtain from successfully completing the race, have become personalized "accidents."[20]

In the fifty years since the "racecourses of the mind" thesis was advanced, universities have undergone rather massive changes. They have become ever more corporate with their ties to business-funded building and research sponsorship; their privatization of research findings; their growing ranks of administrators charged with recruiting funds and bookkeeping tasks while overseeing faculty diminishment with regard to retaining and hiring full-time faculty members; their research-funding emphasis that contributes greatly to teaching negligence with respect to tuition-paying students turned consumers; their use and abuse of part-time sessional faculty and internet technology on the way to becoming "all-adjunct" diploma mills, more interested in certification profits that flow from credentialed training than in education; their magnified glorification of weekly sports spectacles to attract high-school applicants and alumni money; and so on. In all of this, professionalism remains an enduring focal point in the academic world.

In a 2015 article in the Canadian Sociological Association's house journal, Antony J. Puddephatt and Neil McLaughlin, ruminating on "institutional ambivalence and the future of Canadian sociology," provide what is in effect a "racecourse" update on professionals and professionalism, reflecting the rather massive changes as universities have become ever more corporate. In doing this, Puddephatt and McLaughlin note the push and pull between two poles of four continuums of knowledge production: professional versus public/policy sociology; interdisciplinary versus discipline-based research; political versus analytical scholarship; and legal/national versus global audiences. Their argument that "the best way forward" involves "recognizing the ambivalence of our discipline and keeping these conflicting strains in tension"[21] leans heavily on reproducing the professional status quo. They urge us to continue maintaining and policing the intellectual borders of sociology, "a pluralist discipline" that should be governed by the authority of certified professional experts. The authors join those who are "critical of the room for amateurism and lack of standards that can result from the lack of qualified expertise brought to the table by disciplinary experts."[22] Their "standards" argument leads them to be concerned over "the danger" of losing "political" autonomy[23] – which was, as we've already seen, a lost cause – or at least severely eroded. They also expressed concerns over the rise of politically driven approaches in academia: "Political energy has to be balanced with a disciplined, analytical or empirical approach *for the sake of scholarly integrity and credibility.*"[24] While this may well be just another way for them to assert the old notion of scholarly objectivity (without questioning from what quarter this integrity and credibility emanate), clearly the professionalism of experts played a significant role in their deliberations.

The Puddephatt-McLaughlin argument places too much emphasis on "traditional academic standards of peer review" as the insurance that ensures "quality control." They focus on a reward structure for Canadian sociology that might take into account the complexities of the experts' research, but in the final analysis they warn that we "must be careful to discern the quality and credibility of these new open-access journals." They argue for the establishment in that "there must be evidence of publishing in core sociological journals," and urge researchers to avoid "vanity presses' in favour of "the best peer-reviewed university-based and high-quality commercial presses."[25] Their general argument for a middle ground or middle-of-the-road solution to the tensions they analyze does offer guidance in rethinking the discipline of sociology; but it does so in a manner that leaves the disciplined professionalized expertise of the status quo intact, thereby privileging social control and reform over the always disruptive alternatives of progressive social change.

In the end, the Puddephatt-McLaughlin discussion reinforces the dominance of the "expert society" – which just happens to be the title of a book making a similar argument but issued more than sixty years earlier, in 1962. That book, by the respected sociologist Burton R. Clark, a contemporary of the racecourse theorists Jencks and Riesman, foreshadowed their orientation in its service to the status quo. In Clark's reckoning education is becoming "active"; the passive and traditional service function that had made schools "society's main vehicle of cultural indoctrination" was supplemented by education that is innovative – an "active force." Thus, Clark's colleges and universities, because they play an increasingly large part in creating the "expert society" they serve, are becoming, as Jencks and Riesman would later argue, increasingly autonomous.

This autonomy is necessary if higher education is to remain an "active agent." According to Clark, both professors and students are becoming increasingly important interest groups, and in advancing his own racecourse view he sees the development of the academic disciplines as being vital to the restructuring of society. Moreover, he argues that the research orientation of professional educators, when combined with the tolerant attitudes they teach their students, is not only able to create "new culture" but also capable of sustaining the culture it creates. Clark contends, then, that pluralism, the supposedly increased differentiation brought about by the proliferation of academic disciplines, can provide both creative and maintenance functions – but only if professional educators are allowed to develop their academic specialities with a minimum of outside interference. The same pluralism that strengthens professionalism in order to solve problems within the educational institution can also solve the problems of the larger socio-economic order, as objective (that is, professional) educational leaders "steer change in desired directions."[26]

One way of steering change is to block it in a way that protects both what remains of academic autonomy and the hierarchical social-class arrangements of status quo capitalism. Professional academics play their part in blocking fundamental social change, for instance, by learning how not just to bemoan but to manipulate the supposed debilitating tension between two important reference groups, the professional and the bureaucratic. Where student concerns arise, professorial skill in switching reference groups can frustrate and block the questioning of practices and calls for change.

When democratic involvement in departmental affairs – attendance at faculty meetings, development of curriculum, evaluation of professorial classroom performance, hiring of new faculty – becomes the student issue, faculty members can solidify their position within the academic hierarchy by calling on the canons of professionalism to provide them with a rationale for questioning the professionally uncertified students' competence as participants. When class attendance, formal examinations, or grading become of concern to students, the faculty can shift responsibility from their professional selves to the rules and regulations of the academic bureaucracy without threatening their own status. If the professors are adept at playing this game of switching reference groups, they can, in both instances, force students to direct their complaints and animosities elsewhere (in the first instance, "the profession," and in the second case, the academic bureaucracy – "the organization") – in directions that are so complex and amorphous that they severely constrain the students' power to change academic structures. While some potential for conflict does admittedly exist within the academic profession – between the "community of scholars," as both idea and organization, and the reality of academic bureaucracy – the word *potential* here is key: in their daily activities college and university faculty members attempt to ensure that the dialectic between destruction and preservation of this "dual" structure works to their benefit.[27]

Skill in the switching of the reference group not only is a useful way of pacifying students – but can also be a means of confronting administrative and staff requests, requirements and demands, and opposition from a few recalcitrant faculty. It can also provide a way of dealing with various non-professionals and their organizations outside the academic cloister. Skilled employment of this tactic allows professors and allied professionals to continue to frustrate and block attempts at significant social change; it also helps them to protect their supposed autonomy and professional neutrality as expert advisors and consultants.

Given the monopolizing position and power of professional culture, the advice and analysis of experts might well be taken with the proverbial "grain of salt." They have their own interests to look after – chief among them a desire to protect their own positions within prevailing socio-economic arrangements. Continuing to believe in their so-called autonomy while holding on to some version of their supposed professional objectivity permits sociologists and others, in the words of sociologist and critic Alvin Gouldner, "to think of sociology as a way of getting ahead in the world by providing them with neutral techniques that may be sold on the open market to any buyer."[28]

The buyers are a small group of wealthy capitalists who would like their corporate conglomerates to achieve even greater concentrated control of the knowledge industry worldwide – whether in Calcutta, Tokyo, Beijing, New York, or elsewhere. They educate and employ expert scientists in their schools and research foundations – scientists whose continued employment often depends upon learning how to discipline their science with the canons of professionalism that can fire off cannons of another kind. For at times the dictates of global capitalism force multinational corporations to literally bomb people into compliance with corporate needs. It is on these occasions that the corporate owners must find especially comforting the sociology that Nicolaus described as "the official view of the social scene," which continually re-creates anew a cycle of servility.

For their part, social scientists are made comfortable – being handsomely rewarded by the elite for their attempts to shift responsibility for "social problems" from these powerful few and the specific socio-economic arrangements they control to the failings of specific problem individuals and a not-so-specific entity known as "society."[29] This same moralistic reasoning concerned with security and order can not only fix inner-city problems and keep the lid on campus unrest and conflict, but also be transferred over to more global matters such as hunting down international "terrorists," stabilizing "unstable" governments and regimes worldwide, and showing the way forward to struggling economies of "developing" nations. Social science experts have a role to play as technicians who, to borrow a phrase from Noam Chomsky (as relevant today as it was nearly fifty years ago), use their expertise to support "a technology of social tinkering" both domestically and on an international scale.[30]

This social tinkering is encouraged by a scientific professionalism of expertise that quite simply "places the scientist in a moral vacuum."[31]

Tinkering and moral vacuums go together quite nicely. Indeed, many of today's social scientists continue to take their lead from Max Weber, who paid little attention to who was controlling the modern concentration of "the means of production" but was content to build his sociology around the view that forms of state should be seen only (or simply) as "techniques" – that is, as structures ripe for social adjustment.[32] The autonomous expert tinkerer becomes increasingly non-responsible, and eventually irresponsible, with respect to the results of how scientific findings and expert advice come to bolster or alter the social environment. Chomsky elaborates on this question (clearly and concisely) when he argues that this attitude of non-responsibility permits most scientists to believe that there is "no further need for ideologies that look to radical change. The scholar-expert replaces the 'free-floating intellectual' who 'felt that the wrong values were being honored, and rejected the society,' and who has now lost his political role (now, that is, that the right values are being honored)."[33]

Despite the recent movement towards a more public sociology,[34] academic socialization and its racecourse professionalism continue to rule the day. The analysis and understanding of the social world of many of the so-called experts, if not value-neutral, tend at least to be dependent upon the application of proper technique(s) serving to uphold discipline standards and status quo arrangements. As Nicolaus notes in deliberating on the self-serving abdication of social responsibility, with specific reference to the lack of accountability in sociology: "In the last analysis, the only moves toward liberation within sociology are those which contribute to the liberation *from* sociology. The point is not to reinterpret oppression but to end it."[35]

FIVE

Edubusiness and Edutainment

Wealthy Benefactors and Sporting Contributions to the Campus Party

I n a 1989 in-house publication Michael Locke, a distinguished Killam Fellow and professor of zoology at Canada's University of Western Ontario, shared his concerns over the edubusiness direction that his university was taking. His opening paragraph succinctly states:

> I have written this paper because of my deep concern at the neglect of academic quality in our university with the rise of 'edubusiness.' Edubusiness assesses the value of a university to society in figures on its balance sheet with the short term objective of feeding its graduates into the job market. A university sees its mission in the triumvirate of teaching, research, and public service, with the long-term objective of giving people the tools with which to think.[1]

Locke offers several specific examples of how life at his university had suffered as "academics in positions of authority" were "replaced by managers." These "would be business executives," he says, see "no distinctions between administrative units created for convenient service, and academic disciplines without which a university does not exist."[2] Coinciding with the decline of academic influence, the rise of edubusiness, which is in itself bad business characterized by many new and costly inefficiencies, has severely damaged the quality of education.

For Locke, the values of the corporate edubusiness university with its undervaluing of faculty and its business-like servicing of students viewed as consumers were clearly revealed "in the accommodations" provided to "its scholars compared to those occupied by its managers." It is a reality that reflects "the contrast between the offices of business executives and the workers on the factory floor." The managers get "large airconditioned rooms, wall to wall carpeting, modern furniture, coffee tables with magazines, secretarial help with the latest word processors." Most of the faculty members at Western got "12′ × 12′ cubicles, foul air, old issue desks and chairs on hard floors." Adding to the insult, they had "to bring in outside grants to pay for their operations."[3]

Locke reminds readers that his purpose is "not to list inadequacies in our university, but to show how academic decline is linked to changes in the purpose of a university motivated mainly by business style self-interest."[4] He emphasizes how a proper management should serve – and be viewed as serving – the university, as a means to an end and not an end in itself. He closes his paper with a nautical metaphor, assuring readers that his critique is "not a negative attempt to rock the boat. It is a suggestion to the captain that ship's pursers and chandlers should not be in charge of navigation."[5]

Yet even a cursory look at the historical development of Canadian and U.S. higher education would raise considerable doubt as to exactly who is captain of the university ships so routinely kept afloat by wealthy philanthropists and their successful business corporations. History further suggests that those often unwieldy vessels generally steer a course determined by their wealthy benefactors.

The Beginnings of Corporate Edubusiness: A Brief Historical Review of Early University-Business Connections

Some four decades ago in her doctoral dissertation, York University sociologist Norene Pupo wrote about the University of Waterloo's co-operative education program in which students were travelling between the campus and work sites in alternating terms.[6] Such a program was the realization of liquor baron Samuel Bronfman's dream that "the path between the campus and the plant should be open and unhindered."[7] Paving such a path in the postwar period was a huge increase – 405 per cent between 1956 and 1960 – in business and industrial grants to Canadian universities.[8] As Pupo demonstrates, this mid-century increase was simply a highlight dose of a long-running development in which financiers ("big men dealing with larger affairs") made sure that the dictates of piety were suited to or supplanted by the dictates of profit in shaping both school curricula and the evolving social conscience. In her brief sketch of corporate-university relations in Canada over the past 200-plus years, she states (and I quote at length):

> As the modes of production underwent significant transformation from independent commodity production to the later stages of competitive capitalism and monopoly capitalism, universities responded by changing curricula, admission policies, general outlook, and purposes. For example, during the early 1800s, universities were mainly responsible for training clerics and educating sons of the dominant class. Common educational ideas during the time, as espoused by prominent educators and administrators, such as John Strachan and John G. Simcoe, proposed that institutions of higher learning function as socialization agencies to preserve and maintain close ties with Britain. This ideology served the dominant class, the Family Compact, which depended on the British connection for its power, position, and wealth.
>
> By the 1850s, changes were evident in the Canadian social structure as a result of the reform era. Pressure was brought to bear on universities to revise classical and often times religious curricula. Programmes were broadened to include more pragmatic, rational, and scientific subjects, and teaching methods took on new dimensions as instructors moved to demonstrative teaching techniques. Increasingly, members of the dominant class expressed great interest in higher learning. For example, close connections were maintained between William Gooderham, William McMaster, Sir Edmund Walker, John Hoskin, and the University of Toronto, and Peter Redpath, William Molson, William C. MacDonald, and McGill University. These men not only provided funds for the colleges but also sat on the major decision-making bodies of universities. . . .
>
> It was not until 1906 that the Canadian state fully legitimated this relation [between universities and the socio-economic order] with passage of the University Act. Subject to debate for many years, this Act empowered the government to appoint for each university a separate Board of Governors which was to make decisions regarding financial matters. A second body, the university senate, whose members were to be internally recruited from professorial and administrative staff, was to direct policy decisions. However, rules made at this level were subject to the Board of Governors' approval. The ideological justification for the Act was that state supported universities should serve "society at large" and a government appointed body was entrusted to ensure this. In reality, the measure tightened capitalist hegemony in higher education.[9]

As Pupo emphasizes, the case of co-operative education at Waterloo points to a profitable lesson learned early on by governing-class trustees who recognized the benefits of "'socializing' the costs of maintaining schools, universities, and other aspects of the superstructure. . . . Overhead, 'risks' of production, and costs of research and training are diverted to the public sector while benefits and financial gains are accumulated within the private sector."[10]

The growth of colleges and universities in the United States, something I have been researching and writing about since the early 1970s, follows a similar developmental path to that in Canada.[11] Universities have transformed themselves in accordance with and to accommodate the changing needs of the socio-economic system that dominates their continued maintenance and development. A key has been the transformation of university curricula from a classical to a more practical, vocational orientation. Growth of American higher education since the early nineteenth century was dominated by a wealthy few (a socio-economic elite) capable of defining their pursuance of personal interests as being compatible with the best interests of the general public.

The years between 1780 and the beginning of the Civil War saw the founding of nearly one thousand colleges; and selectively bestowing their riches upon particular institutions, a small number of wealthy capitalists decided which few schools among the many were to survive.[12] The price of survival for the "naturally selected" colleges was the continued development of a practical curriculum, a course of study reflecting the discovery by the wealthy few that they might profitably apply a useful science to the technical problems encountered in operating their manufacturing and industrial concerns. Thus, successful capitalists such as Charles Goodyear and later the Armours, the Dukes, and George Eastman hired professors to come up with innovations around, for instance, the possible uses of rubber, and in finding scientific solutions to the problems of producing various consumer goods from hot dogs to cigarettes and cameras. While the professors acted as consultants, college and university administrators sought financial aid for their schools from the wealthy manufacturers and industrialists. Among nineteenth-century college presidents, Harvard's Edward Everett and Brown's Francis Wayland were two of the most successful fundraisers and outspoken advocates of the view that classical curricula should be made pragmatic – that is, profitably modern. They were eventually joined by Dartmouth's Nathan Lord and Michigan's Henry Tappan, staunch supporters of the classical tradition, whose views gradually changed to match their first-hand instruction in the economic reality of the growing educational-industrial partnership.

A particularly glaring example of just how forthright this instruction could be comes from the Philadelphia metal manufacturer Joseph Wharton – and it reflects the inequity of the partnership and the capitalists' desire to strengthen the corporate model by which they were profiting. In an 1881 letter to the University of Pennsylvania trustees, Wharton expressed his concern that "college education did little toward fitting for the actual duties of life any but those who propose to become lawyers, doctors, or clergymen," and he offered his financial aid in the founding of a School of Finance and Economy, provided that it taught particular views.[13] Wharton's desire to see a special emphasis placed upon teaching the necessity of a protective tariff sprang from his support for the corporate ideology of the new capitalism, which was designed to protect his interests in zinc, nickel, and iron. While most wealthy capitalists were less obvious than Wharton regarding the purposes of their educational philanthropy, they were no less concerned about shaping institutions of higher learning so that their curricula would strengthen the corporate partnership between education and industry.

This partnership developed rapidly during the late nineteenth century and early twentieth as Wharton and the elite, a governing class, supplemented their personal gifts to particular schools with Carnegie-style foundation grants and contributions – all of which served to refashion universities into training grounds and giant personnel offices for the scientist-technicians needed to operate the industries. The elite were given political sanction and impetus with the U.S. federal government's passage of the Morrill Land-Grant College Act in 1862, along with later related legislation, whereby the government in Washington agreed to give land to those states that constructed agricultural and mechanical colleges. The result was a tremendous growth that further secularized curricula, moving it away from a clerical perspective in both management and content. This growth also increased the dependency of universities on the prosperity of business and industry, turning professors into knowledge entrepreneurs who either toed and toadied up to the corporate line – or found themselves muzzled.

Corporate Control of Governance in the Edubusiness University: Some Academic Freedom Cases, Past and Present

For those who resisted the push and pull of this trend by causing trouble over university governance policies and threats to academic freedom, punishments ranged from ostracism-type disapproval to dismissal. Prominent capitalists were not about to countenance attacks on the economic structure that they built and dominated. Advocacy of wholesale and controversial reforms of capitalism, along with perceived lesser slights, were met with harsh retribution.

Perhaps the most written about and famous case of interference with regard to university governance and academic freedom occurred a century ago in the case of economist-sociologist Edward (E.A.) Ross at Stanford University. Ross was a member of a group of economists seeking to influence public policy with their challenges to laissez-faire capitalism. According to historian Neil W. Hamilton, "Ross had campaigned vigorously for free silver, a ban on Asian immigration of low-cost labor, municipal ownership of utilities, and public scrutiny of railroads." Hamilton tells how Jane Lathrop Stanford, widow of the California rail baron Leland Stanford and sole trustee of Stanford, believed that such views "compromised the university" funded by her husband. She worked on the university president, David Starr Jordan, to force Ross to resign. He did so in 1900, making sure to give his side of the story to the press. "In response, Jordan indicated that Ross had been forced to resign because of his 'slangy and scurrilous' ways of speaking and not for the substance of what he had said, and that Ross had worse but unmentionable faults that the administration could no longer bear. Jordan asked the faculty to pledge loyalty to the president or risk reprisals."[14]

Jane Stanford's wishes – or, we could say, orders – had carried the day. In the aftermath, one faculty member was fired for defending Ross and seven others resigned. In December 1900 the American Economic Association launched an investigation, and its inquiry found that the charges against Ross were without foundation. The case would later be both instructive and instrumental in creating the American Association of University Professors (AAUP) and in the formation of a principled position regarding academic freedom.

Among the many more recent academic freedom disputes over the last century is the case of University of Colorado professor Ward Churchill. In the years following the September 11, 2001, attacks on the World Trade

Center and the Pentagon, many academics offered comments critical of both previous and ongoing actions of the U.S. government. Churchill was one of the most vocal of the critics. His views become prominent when in several public forums and news media outlets he elaborated upon a published essay and his contention that these attacks on the United States were provoked by U.S. policies abroad. Without abandoning his provocation thesis, he also was careful to make clear that he thought the attacks were unjustified. Even so, the university fired Churchill in 2007 for what it called "research misconduct," and made the charge stick when he appealed and lost a wrongful termination lawsuit.[15]

Canada too, like the United States, continues to have its fair share of politicized edubusiness interference with the academic freedom of university professors. One of the most prominent cases, involving historian Frank Underhill, dates back to the 1930s and 1940s. While Underhill's socialist politics were of the time and not progressive enough to include an equal or equitable place for women,[16] the political tenor of his comments and his involvement with the League for Social Reconstruction and the Co-operative Commonwealth Federation (CCP) almost led to him being expelled from his position at the University of Toronto. Tired of the hassles and long-running disputes with the university, he eventually left Toronto and later joined the Carleton University faculty.[17]

In the 21st century this discordant tune, an inharmonious mix linking corporate interference and university affairs, turned up in two recent and well-known cases at Canada's wealthiest institution of higher learning, the University of Toronto. After U of T hematologist Nancy Olivieri expressed questions and doubts about the efficacy and safety of an experimental drug, deferiprone, which she was testing on behalf of a major drug manufacturer, the pharmaceutical giant – Apotex – went on a campaign to silence and discredit her. The result was a filing of suits and countersuits. When she turned to her employers at the Hospital for Sick Children and University of Toronto for support in this ongoing battle, she was rewarded for her painstaking research by being fired as the director of the hospital's hemoglobinopathy program. As I concluded in another context:

> The university's lack of support became more understandable when it was revealed that it [the school] was in the middle of negotiations with Apotex for a generous financial donation. University president Robert Pritchard went so far as to lobby the federal government with regard to pending changes in drug-patent regulations that might negatively affect Apotex's

bottom line, potentially jeopardizing the building of a new university medical center. In the end, after nearly a decade of tireless struggle Olivieri's actions were vindicated and her besmirched professional reputation at least partially restored in a court-mandated settlement.[18]

Patient safety concerns and academic freedom were also centre stage in the case of psychiatrist David Healy. Following his recruitment from Britain to take over as head of the Mood and Anxiety Disorders Clinic at one of the University of Toronto's affiliated hospitals, the Centre for Addiction and Mental Health (CAMH), Healy gave a public speech in which he was critical of the drug Prozac, warning of safety concerns and the possibility of side effects leading to suicide. In short order, his appointment offer was withdrawn, followed by an announcement that the U.S. global pharmaceutical company that makes Prozac, Eli Lilly, had donated $1.5 million to CAMH and that the new wing of the hospital named after it was now open for business. The various connections involved in this roller-coaster tale of almost-hiring and firing are obscure, but in this case, as in the Olivieri situation, one thing is relatively certain:

> The university as an organization is not simply a passive receiver of corporate philanthropy. Rather, it is an active player in reproducing prevailing corporate arrangements, even at the expense of violating widely recognized and accepted canons of scientific research by ignoring appropriate confidentiality safeguards as well as selectively censoring and delaying the timely full release of research findings.[19]

Another recent case – that of Arvind Gutpa's unexplained resignation as president of the University of British Columbia (UBC) – also raised questions about university governance and academic freedom. Jennifer Berdahl, the 2014 inaugural Montalbano Professor of Leadership Studies at UBC's Sauder School of Business, felt the weight of corporate dominance and gender wrath when in a blog post she speculated regarding Gutpa's departure, writing that he may have "lost the masculinity contest among the leadership at UBC, as most women and minorities do at institutions dominated by white men." She was subsequently phoned by John Montalbano, the man responsible for establishing the professorship bearing his name. In 2014 Montalbano was CEO, RBC Global Asset Management (he retired in 2015). According to Berdahl, Montalbano was highly critical of her comments, saying that they harmed the board's reputation, which is no doubt true. However, he also went on to note that the statements raised questions about her credibility as an academic and, in what can understandably be interpreted as a thinly veiled threat, jeopardized her RBC funding. Berdahl, for her part, refused to retract her blog post and says: "The questions I raised about organizational culture, diversity, and leadership were directly related to my field of study and to my mandate to help organizations advance gender and diversity in leadership, yet I never in my life felt more institutional pressure to be silent." After many weeks of being muzzled, forced by the university to remain silent and unable to defend herself against others' charges and derogatory remarks about her and the work she was doing, a fact-finding report released in October 2015 vindicated her position.[20]

In December 2015 another case came to the fore, this one involving the University of Calgary and its corporate ties to the energy giant Enbridge. The controversy started with a Canadian Broadcast Corporation (CBC) investigation revealing that Enbridge might have been guilty of interfering in the affairs of the university's Centre for Corporate Sustainability shortly after providing a donation. The CBC obtained emails showing that Enbridge sought to influence decisions involving the Centre's board membership and staffing as well as student awards. It might appear that university president Elizabeth Cannon has experienced a particularly rewarding kind of sustainability, a potential conflict of interest kind, whereby she received $130,500 in 2014 in her role as a director of Enbridge Income Fund Holdings. The university's board of governors decided that it would lend a hand in judging these matters by announcing an independent review of the charges, the details of which (implementation date, terms of reference, name of investigator) were not made public at the time of the announcement. The traditional "arms-length" nature of such an in-house investigation is open to speculation – so much so that the Canadian Association of University Teachers (CAUT) has reported that it is likely to initiate its own independent inquiry.[21]

CAUT itself has apparently recognized the manner in which edubusiness corporate learning masquerading as universities continues to alter the state of higher education in Canada. In a late 2015 issue of its *Bulletin*, president Robert Vose notes the growing corporate presence on university and college governing boards during a period in which government funding has dramatically declined, from 80 per cent of total university operating revenues in 1990 to less than 55 per cent by 2012. Bemoaning what CAUT characterizes as "secret agreements, generous payoffs, mysterious resignations, gag orders and cover-ups" plaguing

Canadian universities increasingly dependent on private funds, Vose urges his members to "recognize and confront the resulting contradictions." Politely referring to "the spectre of conflict of interest" raised by public-private research collaborations," he is perhaps somewhat less than fully aware that this shadow threat has become a daily university reality that is proving damaging to much more than research. Despite his admirable call for governance by "clear, transparent, enforceable agreements that protect the principles of academic freedom and autonomy,"[22] Vose, a specialist in medieval history, may, like many others, not fully appreciate the extreme difficulty of this task given the recent alterations in the power structures of higher education in Canada and the United States. The old saw applies: "He who pays the piper calls the tune."

Charles Koch and His Brothers: A Lesson in How Higher Education Corporate Philanthropy Works

All of these cases underscore the dependence of higher education on corporate funding and the many ways in which business dominance plays out on campus as universities knuckle under to the dictates of the corporate piper. *Dark Money: The Hidden History of the Billionaires Behind the Rise of the Radical Right*, by Jane Mayer, and a compelling review of that same book by Connor Gibson, reveal the strength of this corporate stranglehold on U.S. colleges and universities.[23] Mayer profiles the Koch brothers, paying special attention to Charles Koch, starting with Koch industries (with interests that include coal, minerals, fertilizers, pollution "control" technologies, and forest and other consumer products). She details their lengthy history of pollution cover-ups, union-busting and battles with workers seeking wage and benefit improvements. With the death of their father, Fred Sr., in 1967, the four brothers needed to find a way of avoiding paying inheritance taxes on hundreds of millions of dollars. The "charitable lead trust" they set up answered their tax problems but compelled, actually mandated, philanthropy. The mandate for Charles Koch became based on his interest in higher education as a means of pursuing his own right-wing agenda. His educational philanthropy, as Mayer emphasizes, became an extension of his foundational belief that the best interests of the public can and should be equated with furthering his own private interests, a page torn from the history of the nineteenth-century capitalists' playbook. Koch focused on controlling U.S. college campuses, disregarding basic tenets of academic freedom and faculty-shared governance, in servicing his general plan of increasing corporate influence in the society at large.

In a 1974 speech as chairman of the Institute for Humane Studies (IHS), Charles followed the lead of his father and Supreme Court Justice Lewis Powell, who believed that communists had secretly taken over U.S. college campuses. His conservative agenda and philanthropic intentions were clearly joined at the hip as he noted, "We have supported the very institutions from which the attack on free markets emanate. . . . We should cease financing our own destruction . . . by supporting only those programs, departments or schools that 'contribute in some way to our individual companies or to the general welfare of our free enterprise system.' "[24]

Charles began his higher education philanthropy in 1976, using the universities as propaganda machines for his interests. By 2014 he had stepped up his giving. According to a review by Greenpeace of the Internal Revenue Service (IRS) filings from Koch's non-profit foundations, he gave George Mason University (where IHS is now located), the IHS, and the Mercatus Center (a Koch-style think tank that shares a building with IHS) some $77.6 million in foundation money, more than three-quarters of the $109.7 million he had spent on 361 campuses since 2005.[25]

Attempts to root out and crush campus communism, attended by racism and Nazi-style organizing of university students to create a conservative group identity: these are perhaps the expected outcomes, part of Koch's ideological commitment to the so-called "free markets" that allow capitalist socio-economic arrangements to dominate and expand. The details of how this ideological schooling is accomplished are interesting, if a bit draconian. For example, the manner in which the IHS creates and monitors student political views brings to mind the 1880s and the Wharton School's teachings regarding the protective tariff. As Mayer notes: "To the dismay of some faculty members, applicants' essays had to be run through computers in order to count the number of times they mentioned the free-market icons Ayn Rand and Milton Friedman. Students were tested at the beginning and the end of each week for ideological improvement."[26] All of this was part of a "beachheads" strategy that pushes particular ideas onto campuses where they will become prominent in student thinking, an approach practised by Koch, John Olin and his foundation, and several other conservative wealthy benefactors. As the title of Gibson's review correctly puts it: "To Charles Koch,

Universities Are Propaganda Machines." Perhaps the biggest part of getting his message out on the 361 campuses he has some control over rests on the shoulders of those professors he is able to entice with research and grant money to get on board as "free market" lobbyists.

A second blog post by Gibson reviews examples that Mayer provides of professorial lobbyist activity going back to the 1960s, showing that "Koch-funded operatives and professors know that they are in the business of deceiving others."[27] The goal is to gain ideological control of the universities, and as early as 1976 libertarian George Pearson, one of Koch's closest advisors, outlined the control strategy. Former George Mason professor Clayton Coppin summarized the strategy: "It would be necessary to use ambiguous and misleading names, obscure the true agenda, and conceal the means of control."[28] Pearson's suggestions for funding private institutes within universities would have an impact on hiring and other important decisions while hiding the conservative radicalism of donors. More traditional funding schemes such as named chairs would be set aside in favour of what James Pierson of the William E. Simon Foundation and the Manhattan Institute outlined: a control strategy whereby conservative donors look for like-minded faculty whose influence could be enlarged by outside funding, setting them up not in traditional disciplines and departments but, rather, in research centres and institutes that "define[d] programs in terms of fields of study" or could be blessed with "a philosophical or principled identity by giving it the name of an important historical figure, such as the James Madison Program [in] American Ideals and Institutions at Princeton University."[29] For the most part Koch and his donor partners – who have set up their operations on several dozen campuses across the United States – preferred neutral-sounding names for these "research" centres and institutes. Gibson provides a number of examples: the Center for the Study of Economic Liberty, Arizona State University, $5 million co-financed with the W.P. Carey Foundation; Center for the Philosophy of Freedom, University of Arizona, $2.5 million co-financed by Ken and Randy Kendricks and Karl Eller; Institute for the Study of Free Enterprise, University of Kentucky, $12 million co-financed with Papa John's CEO John Schnatter; Center for Enterprise and Markets, University of Maryland College Park, $6 million co-financed with Philadelphia Flyers owner Ed Snider; Center for Free Enterprise, West Virginia University, $5 million co-financed by Ken Kendricks (the strings attached included the school giving the centre a say in hiring the professors funded, which would later prove useful in defending Koch's coal interests in his deregulatory fight over mine safety and clean water standards).[30]

Significantly, the attempt to create neutral-sounding names referring to general fields provides a way of breaking into law schools and other graduate training programs. Piereson underlined the value of this tactic in comments made concerning an Olin Foundation initiative to gain a foothold in legal studies – all of it related to the push by Koch and other wealthy benefactors for a low-regulated or deregulated economy.

> "If you said to a dean that you wanted to fund conservative constitutional law, he would reject the idea out of hand. But if you said you wanted to support Law and Economics, he would be much more open to the idea," [Piereson] confided. "Law and Economics is neutral, but it has a philosophical thrust in the direction of free markets and limited government. That is, like many disciplines, it seems neutral, but it isn't in fact."[31]

In this scheme, "pet" professors are paid to staff neutrally named or "no name" centres and institutes, acting as mouthpieces for Koch's views and passing those views on to hundreds of thousands of university students. It is a formula that has worked well for Koch and associates. Students are not only indoctrinated but also often offered paid internships at Koch-funded advocacy groups. Thus, Koch's influence ranges beyond the university campuses where it had its beginnings. Koch Foundation executives refer to this valuable investment in higher education as "a talent pipeline."

While students in their postgraduate lives are busy spreading the Koch-oriented ideas and advocacy outward from the campus, the pet professors continue to prime the ideological pump with textbooks and Koch-funded reports, using their university affiliations as a stamp of legitimacy and credibility. Gibson cites a couple of Mayer's many telling examples. The textbook in an introductory economics course in the university of the coal-mining state of West Virginia, where Koch industries mine coal, was co-written by Russell Sobel, a former recipient of Koch funding who teaches his view that safety regulations hurt, rather than protect, coal miners. The textbook argues that deregulation is an unmitigated good, and that sweat-shop labour may not be as bad as many think. It forcefully denies that human activities have played any significant role in climate change. When critics have raised objections, the Kochs have characterized the views as providing "fresh" college thinking.[32] At George Mason's Koch-sponsored Mercatus Center, now regularly cited in U.S. Congress documents as a creditable source, more fresh thinking arrived as the Center hired Enron executive Wendy Gramm and then lobbied hard in favour of the Enron deregulation scheme involving oil and gas pipelines. As Gibson adds, "Mercatus also leveraged attacks on President Obama's stimulus package, the plan to spend the economy out of recession."[33]

Given this tangled web of economic and political interests, colleges and universities would be well served in becoming less, rather than more, dependent on wealthy philanthropists. Higher education selling endowments and campus operations to Koch and other private donors may not be good business over the long haul. Increasing dependence on individual and foundation gifts privately bestowed by the wealthy increases institutional vulnerability. Living in constant fear of funding withdrawal is no way to operate, and sliding down the slippery slope of edutainment fun culture is one outcome – which is highly antithetical to a scholarly mission. Yet, given the shaky economics of today's higher learning, it comes as no surprise that universities are broadly welcoming popular culture, and its edutainment aspects, in order to attract potential funding and students.

Edutainment and Advanced Technology: Gaming Culture Moves to the University Classroom

In my book *Fun & Games & Higher Education* I argue that what constitutes the entertainment of sports spectacles on the playing field has moved to the classroom as edutainment. Today's university has to compete with other media-driven institutions, and today's students, growing up in the embrace of a technologically mediated culture that has no historical precedent, expect that their university certification should both not tax them unduly and be entertaining as well. The sophisticated technology that marks the edutainment classroom goes well beyond such minor transformations as blackboard to whiteboard.

The professor's space at the front of the classroom features the replacement of the old-fashioned and outmoded wood lectern with the stainless-steel gleam of a work area that resembles the cockpit of a modern jet airliner with all its bells and whistles. State-of-the-art computerized overhead/power-point projectors and screens are now supplemented with flashing buttons and dials that aid technologist-professors in spicing up their lectures in surround-sound, using film clips, sound bites, and musical accompaniments with webcasts, podcasts, and all that can be found at the ready on the internet. Even the antiquated written words from books, academic journal articles, and more popular magazines and newspapers are available at the flip of a switch. The truly gifted never again need resort to the messiness of chalk or even markers; they have the technology at their fingertips to imitate Steven Spielberg, Martin Scorsese, Sofia Coppola, or any other top movie director. The next hip-hop rock-star professor might not even come from a prestigious school like the University of Toronto but instead might be birthed at the Advanced Technology and Academic Centre (ATAC) building at my own Lakehead University.

To this generation of students I am sure that the jet-cockpit, performance-stage lectern is unremarkable. As "digital natives" they have come of age surrounded by this technology. As they move from game to game and enjoy the many apps on their computers and hand-held devices, their parents' large television- and stereo-centred entertainment den – usually hidden away in a basement rec room – must almost seem a relic of the past. The previous generation's struggle to manipulate the joy sticks that moved Pac-Man (and Ms. Pac-Man) and propelled Mario and other early Nintendo heroes across a series of hurdles and levels must surely be for their kids and grandkids akin to their chimpanzee-like ancestors rising from all fours and discovering fire. Not only have the technological platforms and ease of access changed, but also much of the games' content has been influenced for the better. While the violence and destruction remain ubiquitous, some of the more obvious sexism and racism present in the video games of the 1980s and documented by Eugene F. Provenzo, Jr.[34] have been questioned and removed – which in itself points to the ever-changing restructuring, however incremental and slow, of the social contexts we construct in living our lives. Questioning sexism, racism, and violence, among other issues, is part of a continuing conversation of what we as a society agree to share as appropriate cultural norms – of what we consider to be "normal." These normative definitions, then, change over time and from place to place. Video-game playing and the general idea of "gaming" has much to do with how today's students view higher education and, more specifically, with concerns over "cheating" on college and university campuses.

The prevalent cheating phenomenon has much to do with how many students, and some faculty members as well, see schools and their schooling. As knowledge has become increasingly commodified – a product like any other consumer item for sale – many students have willingly, quite often resignedly, adapted to the role of being consumers of the knowledge industry's offerings. But students are also quite savvy. In recognizing the switch from education as scholarly activity to training courses of pre-packaged information masquerading as knowledge, they understand enough about power to recognize that training, once completed, offers employment-helpful academic certification in the form of societally accepted certificates, diplomas, and degrees. Many of them have critiqued what lies behind this certification process as encapsulated in a belief system that regards society as a meritocracy. They see meritocracy arguments as deficient in failing to give due weight to how so-called "merit" is mediated and often largely determined by ethnic and gender and, perhaps most importantly, social-class differences. Furthermore, the uncovering of these differences, bringing them out of the "hidden curriculum," also sheds light on the ways in which meritocratic belief individualizes and psychologizes school failure while at the same moment protecting the social environment from sustained, change-oriented criticism.[35]

For the students who put together this view of schooling, it is a short step to seeing the entire school certification process as a sham (or a "scam"), a rigged system with a set of graduation requirements worthy of all attempts to beat it or "game" it. What it means to be "honest" and/ or to be a "cheater" in such a system is open to redefinition and refinement, and the accompanying moral compunctions are primed to be re-evaluated. For many of today's students in need of certification for entry-level precarious jobs in an unstable and fast-changing labour market, "gaming" the system is almost mandated and easily justifiable. It is nothing more or less than a video-game victory of a type familiar to them since birth.

Should enterprising students not want to risk facing the unpleasant consequences of getting caught in trying to bolster their academic records on their own, they can always hand off their enterprise and future job potential to the experts. Once at McMaster University I came across a colourful business card, just one among many circulated on campuses, promising in bold lettering "$15 OFF FIRST ESSAY." Underneath it asks, "Do you need to buy an essay?" And in the next sentence commands, "Buy an essay from professionals!" On the other side of the card eHomework provides its website address, lists the many other services available for all coursework (including resumé writing when you're ready to look for a job), and, better still, offers comforting assurance to put the minds of prospective student clients at ease, "You will NOT get in trouble!"

As a culture we have come a long way in refining the practice of cheating since the days of my youth in the 1950s, when we passed crib notes underneath tables and up and down a lengthy row of desks, with several stops and starts timed to coincide with the teacher's changing positions at the front of the class or routine inattention and indifference. Even more recent techniques from the 1990s seem outmoded, archaic today. Take for example, the "stick-shift" technique suggested by Michael Moore (not the famous documentary filmmaker and author), who as an enterprising Rutgers University junior wrote and published *Cheating 101*, a how-to manual extolling cheating as the "easiest and most surefire way of achieving good grades, a diploma, and ultimately a good job." The book was commercially successful, with college-campus sales of over 6,000 copies at $7 each.[36] The stick-shift strategy was designed to help students get the upper hand on multiple-choice tests. Some three or four students who trusted each other would divide up the chapters to be covered by the exam and then look to "the expert" responsible for relevant material for guidance or to any other member of the group who was confident in knowing the right answer and willing to take the lead. If the correct answer was A, the student would place her or his foot where first gear would be on a stick shift, if B, then second gear, and so on through alternative E. It is probably a good thing this technique was derived some thirty years ago as this bit of creativity might never have emerged today, given the decline of the stick-shift manual drive and the digital generation's driving experience limited almost exclusively to automatic transmission options. Still, as they become increasingly immersed in higher learning as edutainment, a lack of familiarity with manual transmissions is no big loss to today's potential cheaters and plagiarizers.

Edutainment as Edubusiness and College Sport as Spectacle: Phil Knight's Nike Philanthropy and Oregon Football

In higher education as edutainment, the gaming phenomenon takes a more literal turn in the manner in which college sports spectacles, with their advanced technology and ubiquitous media coverage, trump academics. The University of Oregon (UO/Oregon) – and especially the spectacular success of its football program – provides an informative case study of this development.

The philanthropy of its most well-known alumnus, Philip ("Phil") Knight, co-founder of Nike, Inc., has rejuvenated UO athletics over the past twenty-some years. Knight has also given hundreds of millions of dollars to Stanford, where he received a degree from its Graduate School of Business, but his wallet and his heart rest with Oregon, where he was born and raised. The son of a lawyer and newspaper publisher, Knight got some practical experience as a sports reporter with the *Oregon Daily Emerald* while earning his bachelor's degree in journalism in 1959. A decent middle-distance runner, he won three varsity letters in track under legendary coach Bill Bowerman, with whom he would later co-found Nike. Upon leaving UO Knight enlisted in the Army, serving one year of active duty and seven more years in the Army Reserve. His Stanford degree led him to work as a Certified Public Accountant and as an assistant professor of business administration at Portland State University.

Following his Stanford graduation in 1962, Knight set out on a trip around the world. One stop was Kobe, Japan, where he was mightily impressed by Tiger-brand running shoes and managed to secure distribution rights to market these "runners" in the western region of the United States. He mailed two pairs to his old coach, who not only gave a ringing endorsement but also made an unexpected offer to partner with Knight. Coach Bowerman had some ideas about design, and the shoe's tread underwent several trials and changes. After seven years and many sales at track meets out of the back of the now infamous green Plymouth Valiant, the original company, Blue Ribbon Sports, took on the now world-renowned Nike name and logo in 1971. Nike, the name of the Greek winged goddess of victory, has flown Knight into rare air, making him a billionaire many times over – at $21.5 billion number thirty-five on the *Forbes* 2015 list of the world's billionaires. Every time Nike sells a pair of running shoes or any of the many items in its diversified product line, the University of Oregon is a potential beneficiary.

Oregon athletics has been especially blessed by Knight's accumulation of riches. In August 2007 Knight announced that he and his wife Penelope (Penny) would be donating $100 million to establish the UO Athletics Legacy Fund, which would help support all athletic programs at the university. At the time this was the largest philanthropic gift in Oregon's history. Later it was matched (2008) and greatly surpassed (2013) by donations to the university's cancer institute in order to fast-track recruitment of scientists and ensure that the latest in technological upgrades would be made available.[37] Technology is a constant theme, present in every philanthropic endeavour that Knight oversees. Oregon football teams in particular have been willing guinea pigs for the latest in breathable, weather-resistant, sleek, and stylish uniforms, equipment, and shoes. The designs, various colour combinations, logo styles, and variations of their game-day attire are the football equivalent to the show-time flamboyant costumes of Las Vegas and are infamous among U.S. college football followers.

Knight's early fascination with running-shoe technology has carried forward to three of his latest projects in support of UO athletics. He put some $68 million into a 145,000-square-foot gridiron football facility, officially opened in July 2013. It is a technologically sophisticated place for sure – showcasing not only a gymnasium with hardwood floors imported from Brazil but also Apple iPhone chargers in each player's locker, auditoriums and meeting rooms with advanced academic technology, and a "game room" for players that includes flat-screen televisions and table football machines.

In 2011 Knight and long-time friend and former Oregon Athletic Director Pat Kilkenny built the Matthew Knight Arena, a new facility for the basketball team. A memorial to Knight's eldest son, who died in a tragic scuba-diving accident at the age of thirty-four, the arena with its 12,000-seat capacity is home to Oregon hoops and volleyball and more – it also has the equipment to stage myriad large-scale entertainment events, everything from scientific and academic conferences to bull-riding, faith rallies, and rock music concerts. The building, a replacement for the venerable but decrepit McArthur Court, was designed to conform to Leadership in Energy and Environmental Design (LEED) standards and in 2013 was awarded LEED Gold Certification. It was the first National Collegiate Athletic Association (NCAA) venue to achieve this status.[38]

Technology in the service of sports science is on full display in a tribute to Oregon's Heisman Trophy–winning quarterback of 2014: the Marcus Mariota Sports Performance Center. The largesse of Phil and Penny Knight provided the $19.2 million that funded this 29,000-square-foot sports-science complex, dedicated to the goal of improving player health. The Center features a neurocognitive facility with the most advanced technology available to diagnose and treat concussions, a persistent and troublesome football injury, along with high-tech equipment to measure and underscore the importance of athlete recovery. It features 3D motion-capture equipment, technology that measures the range of motion in muscles and specifically locates body sites vulnerable to injury. It is high-tech light years beyond the football coach's headsets that Knight likes to wear while watching games from his double suite overlooking Autzen Stadium, the Ducks' home field that he helped to expand with a $30-million gift in 2002. It is the kind of technology that carries the potential not only to optimize athletic performance but also to bolster recruitment efforts – its long-term effect not unlike the indoor weather-protected practice field at the Moshofsky Center adjacent to Autzen, a powerful enticement to lure sun-drenched high-school stars from California and elsewhere who might be reluctant to endure the rain and near-constant drizzle on Oregon's "Wet Coast."[39]

Knight has always been, since his Oregon track days, a loyal Duck sports fan, but the nearly $10 million he donated to make Moshofsky a reality came on the heels of Oregon's 1995 Rose Bowl appearance, the team's first since 1958, and a devastating blowout loss to Colorado the next year in the Cotton Bowl. At that very point, in 1996, Knight decided to underscore his passion for the game, putting his wealth behind taking Oregon football "to the next level." Since the initial Moshofsky gift, Knight has donated more than $300 million to the athletic department. Over the past two decades, the team has appeared in three more Rose Bowls, winning two of them, and in two National Championship games, losing both. In the twenty years from 1995 to 2015, the team failed to be invited to a postseason bowl game in only one year, 2004. During that time the team had a 10-10 won-loss bowl record (including two appearances in the first ever College Football Playoff in 2014–15).

With Knight's boosterism playing an outsized role in producing a perennial nationally ranked football power, Oregon football became something of a Nike branch plant. Knight and several trusted Nike executives set their task as rebranding Oregon football and then selling the team to recruits, fans, and sponsors. As a USA Today sports reporter put it, "At the 1998 Aloha Classic bowl game, Oregon unveiled its new look: dark green, bolder yellow, spiced with black. The aggressive new look conjured images of Star-Wars and superheroes." A Nike executive had also "tinkered with the new logo" – dropping the U and "snazzing up" the O. Not only that, but "The Ducks took the field behind a Harley Davidson."[40] New, more edgy, and stylish uniforms and helmets were added every couple of years. Knight's team, like the facilities he paid for, was modern, shiny, and sleek-looking – maybe even futuristic. Air Jordan in cleats. Oregon rebranded became the place to go for high-school footballers of note, many of whom began to bypass traditional West Coast football schools such as the University of Southern California (USC), UCLA, and Washington, and other powerhouse programs further afield to play for the Ducks.

The Knight push and Oregon football Nike-style were not welcome in every quarter. Some observers noted that Knight had become too close to the team with, among other things, his head-set listen-ins, fill-in meetings with offensive and defensive co-ordinators, on-field presence during pre-game warm-ups, locker-room visitations to socialize with the players, and 2001 push for a Times Square billboard to hype quarterback Joey Harrington's Heisman Trophy campaign. Nike's bottom-line business practices received negative press as the target of global anti-sweat-shop demonstrations and became the focus of protest activity around worker rights.[41] Many consider Knight's Oregon philanthropy as just another bottom-line practice, connecting achievements on the football field and the team's platform as a big-screen display case to the launching and showcasing of Nike products. With Knight, as with other wealthy entrepreneurs, philanthropic and corporate interests no doubt meet and reinforce each other. His wealth permits a unique separation from the crowd, but in his fan interest Knight is not alone. Plenty more folks, much poorer and more ordinary, are willing to join the sports entertainment party.

This pattern, again, is reflected in the tailgate parties that accompany big-time college football, which create both business and social opportunities. The party at the tailgate often wins out over the action inside the stadium, and corporate sponsors often do not even include stadium tickets in the game-day packages they offer clients. Some individuals who have tickets don't bother to enter the stadium, preferring the big-screen televised version and the company of their tailgating friends and family set-up in parking lots near the field of play. This is reminiscent of the earliest U.S. college football games in the mid-nineteenth century, when the sports writers of the time devoted most of their column space to describing who was at the game, with whom they arrived, and their social standing, as well as what kind of conveyance they arrived in and when, along with how they were dressed, what hijinks occurred in the stands, and which fans and how many were arrested for post-game disorderliness. As Michael Oriard has ably argued, it was precisely this lack of attention to what was happening on the field that cemented the collective reputation of early sports reporters as prominent creators who turned college sports into entertainment spectacles.[42] The game spectacles and accompanying parties made billions of dollars for entrepreneurs serving tailgaters' needs, and now college football Saturdays in the United States reach millions of fans through big-screen televisions and computers that enable live streaming. While the before-, during-, and after-game socializing and mingling at tailgate events and at other special locations both on and off-campus are routinely confined to game-day Saturdays, at times the activities can cover a long weekend from Thursday through Sunday evening. Party On!

Although they do not always go together, big-time university sports and big-time partying have become strange bedfellows of a sort. The infamous National Lampoon's *Animal House* movie (1978) was filmed on the Oregon campus – a school highly capable of mixing pigskin excellence with party-pack fun. *The Princeton Review*'s annual ranking of the nation's top party schools, often cited as the most exhaustive and reliable of several such lists, placed Oregon at number 19 in 2014. As reporter Michael Russell phrased it in the *Oregonian* newspaper, in the nationwide survey of 130,000 students the university "crept one beer-soaked rung up" from its 20th-place ranking in 2013.[43] The connection between sports entertainment, in this case college football, and campus partying is perhaps evident in the 2014 top 20, with fully half the schools among the nation's perennial football powerhouses.

At universities everywhere, the party atmosphere has a noticeable effect on Friday and weekend classes. My own experience at Lakehead University – which has basketball and hockey teams but does not field a football team or offer weekend classes – suggests that Friday classes are avoided like the plague. Everyone, students and faculty alike, favours the three-day weekend. While some Friday morning instruction does occur, by noon you could take up bowling in the halls of the building where I taught most of my classes.

Friday class avoidance is not the only way the party alters the classroom. In the ten years since my book *Fun & Games* was published, corporate business concerns and accompanying social aspects have converged further and become more intertwined in the edutainment university. In a general way edutainment has resulted in a quality reduction that is not unlike what has transpired in big-time college football, where the entertainment machine has drastically ramped up the bowl postseason. Where once there were the big four bowls, Rose (the oldest, established in 1902), Sugar (1935), Orange (1935), and Cotton (1937) – and much later the Fiesta Bowl (1971) and a few others – the 2015–16 season offered forty bowl games played amongst some of the eighty teams sporting the NCAA minimum bowl eligibility requirements of at least six wins and a .500 record. (A plan is in place to go even lower, to perhaps five wins and seven losses, if not enough "worthy" teams are available to fill the slate.) In the edutainment era, certification downgrades and quality-control issues are not just football-related but are also moving from the playing field into the classroom. The world of edutainment is clearly at play in corporate universities on both sides of the 49th parallel.

From the Playing Field to the Classroom: The Ever-Widening Circle of High-Tech Entertainment Culture

In recent years even smaller liberal arts universities have jumped onto the increasingly downward slide of higher education into fun culture – taking up, as a popular strategy, the promises of a lusty edutainment.[44] In their attempts to market their discipline to prospective students, several departments have been putting forth the kind of accessible curriculum that might entice busy students who are pressed for time – often holding part-time jobs to cover rising tuition costs – and absorbed with social media as entertainment. As a survey of marketing practice found:

> Programs would promise 'fear, fun, advertising, youth, action film, the entertainment industry, consumerism, and many more.' Another department describes the content as 'cutting edge social issues such as sweat shops, hate crimes, gang violence, professional wrestling.' One department enticingly asks 'What can we learn from watching and analyzing films like Trainspotting?' In short, not only will the degree be easy and accessible, but entertaining as well.[45]

Such marketing attempts indicate more than higher education's transformation to edutainment. They also reveal institutions driven by internal competitions for the administrative funding that is routinely doled out in accordance with enrolment figures and formulas based on student-faculty ratios. Similarly, on an individual instructor level, if professors can make their courses look like "fun" or provide the promise of "a good time," they can improve their chances of securing full rather than prorated pay. Recently, I must admit, the unexpected need to pay for a new roof on my house led me to play this game in a spring-summer course offering, where the professor needs to attract a minimum of fifteen students to receive a full stipend. Fortunately, my third-year course on the "Sociology of Everyday Life" was tailor-made for an edutainment appeal. As the description of the course that would keep my home dry stated:

> This course will focus on how the sociological imagination can offer important insights useful in understanding our everyday/everynight lives. Lectures, discussions and readings will emphasize the interplay between work and leisure to aid students in understanding the importance of class, ethnicity and gender in various settings – on the job, at school, at a sporting event, as car drivers, as users of public transportation and social services, as taxpayers, as contributors to screen culture (users of cell phones, the computer, television and video-games), as shoppers at the mall, as party goers, as patrons of a neighbourhood bar, and so on. All are invited to come to the party, contribute to our discussions and have some fun in school this summer.

The discussions and any fun to be had were only available to those who made time to come to the party. This was an in-person classroom experience where you literally had to be there rather than having your presence simulated and mediated by the high-tech edubusiness world of edutainment. Confusions and differing definitions of what it means to be in the moment are plentiful, and the new technology not only immerses us further in the edutainment maze but contributes much to what many regard as a cheating epidemic in higher education.

A case in point involves cheating on MOOCs (Massive Open Online Courses). As reported in *The Chronicle of Higher Education*, researchers at Harvard and MIT discovered that some students were clever enough to create at least two accounts in a MOOC: "one or more with which to purposely fail assignments in order to discover the correct answers, which they use to ace the assignments in their primary account." The data analyzed came from nearly two million course enrollees in 115 MOOCs offered at the two universities. The researchers found: "More than 1 percent of the certificates earned appeared to result from this kind of cheating. And among those students who have earned 20 or more certificates, 25 percent had used this strategy to cheat."[46] Imagine the possibilities when this tactic and others are transferred to credit-carrying courses.

Cheating can also play a role in course organization and presentation. In "Busted," a review of cheating in Canadian colleges and universities, Kyle Carsten Wyatt argues that academic cheating may be of greater concern than other types of dishonesty and corruption because young people's characters and habits, shaped by their school experiences, influence their adult lives and interactions as they "face the pull of corrupt influences." As illustration he muses: "Ten years from now, the medical student who accepts a bribe may well be a general practitioner prescribing medicine. Will it be the drug that works best, or the one whose pharma rep sent him on a cruise?"[47] In his concern over student ethics, he wonders to what extent college cheating is a "gateway" crime. He uses the example of news media magnate Lord Conrad Black, who was sentenced to federal prison in the United States in 2007 on charges of fraud and obstruction of justice. Wyatt wonders if that life experience had anything to do with Black's expulsion from Toronto's Upper Canada College in 1959 for his youthful entrepreneurship in selling exams.[48]

While cheating among students (plagiarism, "unauthorized collaboration on homework, copying answers, and impersonating someone else on an exam") as self-reported has remained roughly the same at about 75 per cent over the past fifty years,[49] certainly the technology available today to students of situational ethics bent on gaming the system offers options undreamed of a half-century ago. Wyatt supports this point:

> Throughout the twentieth century, students sought ingenious ways to evade detection. In 1965, a Seattle inventor identified a campus market for his battery-operated PockeTutor, a tiny device sold by mail order for $19.95 (US) that promised to "put you at the top of your class" by making notes "easily visible to you, even without others knowing." A wristwatch accessory was offered for an additional $19.95. PockeTutor buyers could only dream of the cheating capabilities of the Apple Watch.[50]

A final group, besides administration marketers and students, affected by edutainment corporate culture in academia and its reliance on advanced technology is made up of the growing ranks of professors known variously as "sessionals," "contract lecturers," or "adjuncts." Much has been written about the abuse this group has suffered as the professoriate's second-class citizens, but I want to emphasize here that their plight is the direct result of corporate edubusiness seeking profit in much the same way as the entertainment industry does. The modus operandi is to hire an army of itinerant lecturers to teach large sections of introductory and lower-level courses at a fraction of what it costs to employ tenure-track and tenured professors. It is not unlike Hollywood's use of "extras," stunt performers, and "doubles" plus high-tech wizardry to simulate locations and action sequences. Yet in the edutainment-edubusiness university, the highly paid stars are often missing – they are off-campus on research, writing, and speaking assignments. The standard salary packages of Meryl Streep, Halle Berry, Angelina Jolie, Jack Nicholson, Denzel Washington, Brad Pitt, and their peers certainly would offer edutainment star power in the classroom, but are out of reach for even the wealthiest universities. If the vocal and acting skills of Hollywood's finest cannot be obtained, perhaps our edutainment universities could make do by increasing the teaching loads of their millionaire football coaches, drawing upon their technological expertise to bring high-tech learning packages and accompanying lecture material to the students. Once again, most obviously, moving entertainment from the playing field to the classroom is not such a big stretch.

Indeed, when the bulk of students arrive at college, they go looking for the sports and the fun. In his book *The Nature of College: College Culture, Consumer Culture, and the Environment*, James Farrell cites an American Time Use Survey of the United States Bureau of Labor Statistics that found that "full-time American college students spend more time on leisure and sports than on classes and homework." Farrell, a U.S. college professor who developed a "Campus Ecology" course that makes students the subjects of their own environmental studies, concluded: "If actions are a measure of values, then college students value fun more than learning." He also cites a survey done by the Pew Research Center. When people ranging from eighteen- to twenty-five-year-olds were asked "to describe their generation," they came up with "labels like 'lazy,' 'crazy,' and 'fun.' Fifty percent of teens told Teenage Research Unlimited (TRU) that their generation is 'about fun,' and sixty-nine percent claimed that they 'always try to have as much fun as possible.'"[51]

Farrell links college/university life as a coming-of-age time of transition to "fun" culture. Shopping (often accomplished online) and occasionally stopping in at the bricks and mortar educational boutique or superstore are for many of today's students activities not far removed from their middle-school and high-school trips to local shopping malls. The social aspects and the potential for fun that accompany these visits to school, or to The Gap or some other commercial outlet, help to turn university students into education consumers who learn to have little regard for the slog of traditional scholarship. The educational managers at McMaster University, for example, make this quite clear as they encourage Mac students to enrol in courses by adding the choices to their "shopping cart."

Farrell is perhaps at his best when he moves from his general comments on fun culture to dissect what he calls "the cultural work of parties." He discusses four party components: the role played by alcohol in "altering body chemistry and consciousness"; "the work-play dichotomy" of the culture surrounding the university as it feeds unconstrained weekend celebrations that offer students a contrast to disciplining professors and their academic disciplines, reminders of the academic work week; "the interplay of boredom and fun" that supports the dialectic of work and play, feeding advertisers whose business is to keep us as a society addicted to novelty and excitement, and to make the wild party "the default option for boredom-beating on campus"; and finally the role played by "a feeling of spontaneity and novelty and contingency," brokered by party conventions that tame the wildness of the party and its transgressions with regard to "the conventional rules of proper social behavior."

Still, as Farrell emphasizes, the wildness of the party "stays entirely within the rules of commercial behavior." These wild parties point to and reinforce a historical pattern of "the commercialization of fun – the creation and commodification of experiences (and audiences) that mark a culture of distraction and pleasure."[52] As in the case of football tailgate parties, the party is certainly not revolutionary, nor even subversive. It is big business, profitable for distributors of beer and snacks, clothing manufacturers, musicians and their producers and promoters, and condom companies. Partying may take a bite out of student budgets, but it is a payday for relevant entrepreneurs. Fun, then, is saleable – but, as Farrell recognizes, happiness is not.

Consequences or Who Pays for the Party: Part-time Non-Tenured Professors and Most of All, Students

In this transformation of the corporate university into a learning centre that features high-tech edutainment, a key question becomes who is *Paying for the Party*, the title of a study by sociologists Elizabeth Armstrong and Laura Hamilton. That both sessional lecturers and students are paying a high price is clear. The research on students reported in Armstrong and Hamilton's book, subtitled *How College Maintains Inequality*, is testimony to the myriad ways in which the edutainment university reinforces and deepens divisions along intersecting lines of social class, gender, and ethnicity. Their research method combines participant observation with qualitative interviews. In 2004 Hamilton, closer to the students age-wise, "settled into a room in a coeducational residence hall at a large research university in the Midwest" to participate first-hand in the college lives of her white, heterosexual, unmarried and childless, eighteen-year-old dorm mates. Initially she was aided by a research team of four graduate students and three undergraduates. Eventually their work would develop into a five-year study, involving forty-eight of the fifty-three women living on a particular floor from whom they obtained subsequent annual interviews as their postgraduate lives unfolded. The importance of social-class differences with regard to both monetary and cultural capital was clearly evident.

The authors outline a major example: a comparison between Taylor and Emma, two of the students observed entering Midwest University (a pseudonym). Both students planned to pursue careers as dentists and had similar high-school grade-point averages or GPAs (although Emma had straight A's and advance placement classes). They came from middle- or upper-middle class families (although Taylor's parents were more affluent), and both chose biology as their college major, with Taylor attaining a higher university GPA. Emma's postgrad job opportunities were constrained by her student loan bill and the economic necessity of having to move back in with her parents in a small "Rust Belt city," where the best and most relevant work she could find was to become a dental assistant at a relatively low hourly wage. Finally, after failing to be admitted to graduate school she sought refuge by marrying her boyfriend of working-class origins and moving onto the military base where he was stationed. This arrangement allowed her to gain access to the spousal health and educational benefits provided by his relatively low-paying job with the military.

Taylor, in contrast, benefited from parental support and graduated debt-free, even though she had to pay out-of-state tuition, and was successful in gaining admission to dental school. Her parents were also prepared, if necessary, to offer further monetary support, allowing Taylor to build upon the cultural capital valuable to adult success that from the beginning had separated her from Emma and her family. Taylor, "enmeshed in a vibrant campus community," could afford to remain single. She was in no rush to marry as she continued to nurture and enlarge a social network that included not only dental student colleagues but also other graduate students similarly situated. As the authors put it: "Taylor appeared on track to reproduce her upper-middle class origins. Emma, conversely, left college at risk of downward mobility. . . . Their fates diverged upon entering the organizational infrastructure of Midwest University. Here, relatively small class differences were magnified, sending them in different directions."[53]

Armstrong and Hamilton's research reveals not only social class differences and their effects but also the "party pathways" of the edutainment university. The girls' participation in the "Greek system" of sororities and fraternities involved a "rush" selection process that emphasizes "peer-driven screening and ranking mechanisms – centred on social ties, personality, sexual reputation, and cuteness."[54] Those girls selected to join sororities become part of an exclusive social circle and are protected in a way that minimizes contact with the "wrong sort" of people. In this social context fraternity boys join the ranks of potential marriage partners, and some of the sorority sisters improve their life chances by dropping their small-town high-school boyfriends, who, as it turned out, came from the wrong backgrounds. This process of selectively removing some parts of the cultural capital brought from home and adding to it in other ways involves redefining and policing expressions of "femininity" with regard to hair style, dress, and manifest expressions of intelligence. For the "socialites" and "wannabes," partying was not just about "having fun" but was instead a "vocation" based upon "the assumption that being really good at being a 'girl' has social value and can be exchanged for certain kinds of career success and – most important – a well-heeled male breadwinner."[55]

In a book review of *Paying for the Party* – entitled "Social Arts Trample Liberal Arts" – Matthew Reisz stresses the effect of this trend on academics. Edutainment majors abound, and for Reisz:

> The reasons for this are not difficult to fathom. Sheer financial pressures on universities make "extremely affluent students with middling academic credentials" very attractive. So institutions lay on a range of "pink-collar" "easy majors," with no Friday classes to interfere with partying, which lead to careers in media, sport or fashion where "appearance, personality, and social ties matter at least as much as [academic success]." "Business-lite" subjects such as recreation sport management and tourism management are "almost exclusively filled by women," and "appeal to the particular kind of upper-middle class femininity that they were simultaneously working to perfect in the party scene."[56]

There is a cautionary note here as the "party pathway" can be a seductive trap with dire consequences. The Armstrong-Hamilton research records several such cases, including a particularly instructive one in which a student from the working class switches majors from education and teaching to tourism and wedding planning. Eventually, too late, she realizes that she will never possess the cultural and social capital of her more privileged classmates, whose social ties and important connections would allow them to succeed, and her lack of same would spell failure in this type of career.[57]

Reisz sums up *Paying for the Party* and the edutainment university:

> What emerges is a trend towards what has been called the "country-clubization" of US universities, where increased spending on student services such as recreation and athletics has greatly outstripped that on academic instruction and financial help for the disadvantaged. For many at "Midwest University," the "college experience" is a bit like a luxury cruise, ideally suited to the privileged and "not quite adult."[58]

College life will always have its social side, and, it seems, parental differences in affluence and the consequences for their children are practically immutable to change. However, changes in the policies and programs put into place by individual universities and governments can alter how intersections of social class, gender, and ethnicity influence student outcomes and life chances. So too can the classroom, as there are many ways in which professors, with encouragement and incentives provided by the university, can creatively organize and present course material. The rise of the corporate edutainment university portends something new and different that goes well beyond the existence of a social side in college life. Then too, the edubusiness-edutainment university has created a different learning context within which academic and scholarly activity takes place – and that is the phenomenon of distance education.

SIX

Educators and Education at a Distance

The High-Tech Classroom and the New Mediated Learning

M y thoughts on distance education and the role of technology in delivering it have not changed much over recent decades. In 1997, in summarizing "the homogenizing computer-driven glut of information" that makes up distance education, I offered a warning about technology-mediated decontextualized learning:

> If we continue pouring resources into an education at a distance centred on the "efficiency" of machine technology our universities will continue to replicate the computerized mentality behind the machine, as well as its learning "outputs." It is an education that will make it even more difficult for students and faculty to learn critical person and place distinctions but also, and more generally, how to critically distinguish the meaningful from the trivial.

My concern then, as now, was that we were well on the road to losing a kind of learning that is central to the purpose of higher education. Part of this same tendency, also, was that education at a distance was aiding and abetting in the loss of other crucial knowledges and skills. "Higher learning shaped in the computer mould of the electronic age [was and is] changing both the character of scholarship and the scholarly climate as it develops in today's universities." The threat seems glaringly obvious: "Electronic 'learning packages' to be 'delivered' at a distance pacify both student and faculty 'consumers' to the teaching and research dictates of the market."[1]

Since the mid-1990s, as a management mentality has become increasingly dominant, market dictation and money-talk have accompanied the growth of distance education. Social historian John Ralston Saul has insightfully characterized the education managers who have risen to prominence within today's universities: "Thought is not a management function. Because the managerial elites are now so large and have such a dominant effect on our educational system, we are actually teaching most people to manage not to think. . . . The teaching of transient managerial and technological skills is edging out the basics of learning."[2]

In a similar vein, in her book on education, *More Money than Brains: Why School Sucks, College Is Crap, & Idiots Think They're Right,* English professor Laura Penny emphasizes the significant differences between print culture and digital culture:

> I love the Web. However, I do not think, like some technoptimists, that skimming blogs or completing a Facebook quiz is equivalent to reading challenging material and learning how to make an argument about it. Rather, unprecedented access to information means that it is all the more urgent that we teach students how to evaluate that information, how to judge the countless claims on sites of wildly varying quality.[3]

Somewhat sadly, the Lakehead University calendar (2015–16) offers a description of Continuing Education and Distributed Learning (CEDL) that is eerily similar to the 1995–96 entry, which not only rationalized distance education as the flexible answer to geographic and employment barriers, but also provided several "convenience" reasons for enrolling in distance education courses.[4] In 1995–96 the enticement of high-tech education appeared as a kind of entertainment forum not unlike the mass media techniques driving popular culture. The university "is pleased to offer . . . the Distance Education mode of delivery [which is] enhanced by audio/video materials and audio teleconferencing."[5] More recent technological advancements have only added pizzazz, more bells and whistles, as well as an E-learning manager, to this older description. But I want to be unmistakeably clear: my point in charting the development of distance education is not to rail against technological innovations and what some might consider the misnomer "social media," but rather to emphasize how technologized schooling decontextualizes and often destroys a particular kind of sociability central to learning as scholarship. As I put it in my 1997 critique of computer-mediated schooling: "Meaning (interpretation, subtlety, historical moment, etc.) is lost as the computer and the zoned or walled microworld it helps produce deny (or often at least attempt to deny) the most fundamental reality of being human: Knowledge is both situationally constructed and continually changing because, like reason and any other human interaction, *it is a social activity.*"[6]

Some of this social activity was lost as Lakehead University championed distance education as a cost-effective, efficient way not only of enticing students from the region who had previously enrolled in distance courses offered by several universities in Southern Ontario but also of serving potential students already enrolled at Lakehead University and living in Thunder Bay.

Education at a Distance versus In-Person Instruction: Continuing Education and Sociology at Lakehead

Lakehead University offered its first distance education course in sociology in the academic year 1988–89.[7] A second-year criminology course attracted seventeen students. In summer 1989, forty-five students signed up for introductory sociology online. From fall 1989 to spring 1990 and then each year through to 1993–94 the sociology department offered four courses through distance education; from 1994–95 to 1995–96 it was five courses, with a spring-summer course to start that May. Enrolment figures for each year from 1989 through 1995 were: 127, 130, 154, 188, 202, 293, and 345 without the spring-summer course. Not only did enrolment rise every year, but with that came an increased demand for a greater variety of courses. During this seven-year period criminology and introductory sociology courses online were joined by a second-year family studies course and third-year courses in the sociology of medicine and work. Apparently student consumers appreciate the convenience of education at a distance.

During that time the continuing education, off-campus, in-person course offerings in sociology declined at a rate mirroring the increases in distance education. In 1988 the department had thirteen off-campus, in-person courses at all year levels, enrolling well over 100 people each year. The following four years (1989 through 1992) saw 9, 10, 10, and 11 sociology courses offered, with a combined enrolment of some 90 students per year. Students from more than a dozen communities were involved, most of them on a continuing basis over several years. Participation was strong enough that both Kenora and the much smaller town of Atikokan were able to acquire the informal designation of a branch campus. By 1993 and 1994 the number of courses had dropped to five each year, resulting in a sharp dip in enrolment, accompanying a severely diminished diversity in offerings (over the entire period 1989–96 nineteen course topics were offered to students). By the academic year 1995–96 not one in-person sociology course was offered by continuing education in the Northwestern Ontario district outside of Thunder Bay.

By no means did consumer convenience and satisfaction constitute the major force behind this change. The economic engine driving the change was cost-profit calculations and government support for expensive high-tech development. Any lingering pedagogical considerations or doubts about moving from in-person instruction unmediated by technology to education at a distance gave way to considerations of "the bottom line." Administrators (educational managers) view education at a distance as costing the university less – which consequently means it generates greater profits. Even so, some economic considerations were not at the time (and never have been) adequately weighed.

The sociology department at Lakehead provides a good illustration of the hardships produced by the narrow economic logic driving education at a distance. In the seven-year period from 1989 to 1996, distance education employed four different instructors to teach sociology courses, with most of the work falling to just one person. During the same period the university employed seventeen different instructors in the continuing education program of in-person instruction. Moreover, the in-person off-campus classes not only provided employment but also a continued learning opportunity for a few Ph.D.s living in Thunder Bay and for several M.A. students who had recently graduated from the department. Over half of those employed – nine of the seventeen – got their first teaching experience, cut their instructor's teeth, in the continuing education program. In a deteriorating economy plagued by joblessness, yet another place to partake of first-time and maybe even continuing employment – a chance to build upon previous learning and skill development – was scuttled. Finally, local economies accustomed to servicing the overnight and weekend needs of the in-person instructors also suffered damage, however slight.

Current funding arrangements and proposals along with developments in e-learning technology favour education at a distance. By the late 1990s in-person, off-campus continuing education had become an ancient relic, and now the only sociology courses offered off-campus taught by in-person instructors on location are financed by and offered in conjunction with the Indigenous people of the Seven Nations. On the

Thunder Bay campus CEDL (Continuing Education and Distributed Learning) has kept its hand in with regard to in-person classroom instruction by offering just a couple of such courses in the spring-summer sessions, a definite minority of the total package of sociology courses offered. Most of CEDL's resources and energy go towards serving the needs of several thousand distant education registrants both on- and off-campus. E-learning and distributed learning cover a variety of disciplines, programs, and faculties, ranging from business and nursing to education and public health. Enthusiasts can obtain an M.A. in public health by taking all of their courses online. The online advertising boasts, "There is no requirement to attend on campus." This experience, again, leads to questions around the sociability upon which scholarly curiosity and creativity depend.

Other consequences arise from the new education at a distance being economically driven. One of them is that those steering the distance education bandwagon might eventually find themselves no longer in the driver's seat. With the elimination of the in-person instruction formerly provided to small-town residents, the question is: what comes next? With technologically mediated instruction purportedly bringing the convenient benefits of individualized course selection and supposed improved quality as well as economic efficiency to the hinterland periphery via the metropolitan core of Thunder Bay, why shouldn't the process be extended even further?

After all, the instructors and students can come from anywhere and everywhere, unencumbered by institutional affiliation and geographic place – anachronisms made nearly meaningless in electronic cyberspace – so then why not join local, electronic education zealots with their counterparts in Toronto? Why couldn't that core metropole do for us in Thunder Bay and maybe for the whole of Canada and the world (see Massive Open Online Courses or MOOCS) what we have so effectively done for the peripheral hinterlands in our Lakehead district? After all, the same arguments of economic efficiency, personalized freedom, and quality would hold in bringing us up to "electronic speed."

In this distance education scenario it might well be the Ministry of Education of the Province of Ontario bringing us up to speed, administering and institutionalizing an expanding education at a distance that would intensify the dismantling of the traditional in-person, classroom-oriented university. If some of us at Lakehead and elsewhere don't like this direction and object, we can and will be forcibly re-educated. Soon enough we might be made to see that certain sacrifices (perhaps exchanging full-time jobs for part-time sessional work or losing jobs altogether) are necessary in order that the slow, too boring, talking-heads tedium of the in-person university can be replaced by the exciting electronic jolts of the high-tech edutainment university at a distance. The government might even be able to secure the services of some high-profile Hollywood actors to speak our professorial parts whenever the old-fashioned lecture format is deemed appropriate.

The issue, again, is that this kind of technologically inspired permeation/coverage decontextualizes and poorly repositions actual learning – making it over in the image of the technology that inspires it.

Knowledge Creation and Scholarship as Social Activity: Sociability and the Role of the Computer in Decontextualizing Higher Education

For most of us, computer technology has already reorganized and reshaped the world we live in. While many people do celebrate this new virtual reality high-tech world, as Canadian communications analyst Bruce Powe warns us, we should critically reflect upon what are defined as its advantages, being careful not to be used by it. For Powe, the computer, along with the telephone, fax, radio, and television, "offer an experience of a kind but it's sensory, it's not existential. You have to be very clear about that distinction. As long as you are aware of the process you can begin to manoeuvre through the thickets of reality."[8] To make this foray we need to get behind the glitz and glitter of computer technology to examine the rationality, the way of thinking, that drives it.

Computer thinking creates a "microworld" of information "bits," exacting formulations formatted for input in a manner compatible with the technology's characteristic binary logic. The microworld is a zone in which data can be classified, judgments made, and output produced in a manner relatively unimpeded by, cleared of, human foibles. Being in this zone means that information is reduced to small atom-like components stripped of interpretive symbols, so that "within computer space nothing out of the ordinary occurs."[9] Actually, for those of us not yet fully resident in virtual reality, in a very real (existential) sense it is just the opposite – very little *within* the ordinary happens, if by this we mean the usual or customary flaws and foibles associated with face-to-face human interaction.

The computerized zone is a "place" in which time and physical conditions stand still, they do not matter – a place with little ambiguity. It is not unlike what sharp-shooting basketball players describe as "being in a zone" – a "place" where crowd noise is shut out, confidence (positivism) reigns supreme, and the basket looks so big as to be almost unrecognizable or unreal. It is a kind of virtual reality – which explains why heavy computer users have a hard time returning from their perfect virtual "highs" to the fuzzy ambiguity of real-world relations. Likewise, it explains why basketball (and other entertainment) stars who regularly find themselves in the zone often have trouble dealing with the ordinariness of everyday reality.

Creating a computerized zone is a kind of decontextualizing that creates a façade of simplicity. Constant heavy showers of computer-generated and -mediated information are to be had in this realm, and Powe speaks for all of us concerned about the "information glut" when he characterizes it as "deeply distracting, overwhelming, confusing."[10] Most importantly, the computer as a technology treats all of this information as being of equal importance – it all seems to come from and often is about nowhere and everywhere at the same time. This decontextualization often makes the "information society" overwhelming and nonsensical.

It is precisely here, in rectifying this computer malaise, that higher education has an important role to play. Colleges and universities should be carrying out their traditional work by using in-person instructors who are presenting and offering critiques of various arguments and interpretations, who are facilitating in-class discussions in face-to-face interaction that engages students and helps them to sort out and separate the meaningful, the important, from the trivial. But instead this crucial social aspect that is vital to the lifeblood of scholarly activity is being lost to both students and professors as the technology-driven education at a distance of edubusiness in the corporate university turns learning into edutainment "learning packages" that are "delivered" by and to "educational consumers." As Theodore Roszak so succinctly put it some thirty years ago in his book *The Cult of Information: The Folklore of Computers and the True Art of Thinking*, "The paramount truth [is] that *the mind thinks with ideas, not with information*."[11] Institutions of higher learning should be helping the mind think, not hindering it.

A tendency to confuse data with information and information with ideas, as well as to be surprised by the reach of technology, is not uncommon. Neil Postman, following in the footsteps of several scholars (including Canadians Harold Innis and Marshall McLuhan), gives voice to this idea of technology's reach with his two-pronged observation: new technology almost always takes over more of the terrain than our expectations allow for; and with the computer, as with every technological innovation, you gain something but lose something as well. His book title, *Technopoly: The Surrender of Culture to Technology*, makes his views clear, as did a 1992 radio interview on CBC's *Morningside*.

In the interview he began by acknowledging that "a computer can do many things" but also noted that "it does change the nature of what we are doing." He told a story about a professor at the University of Texas who was teaching a course in poetry and discovered that the students were rather reluctant not only to read their poetry aloud but also just to talk in class with others. As a solution he had them communicate by means of the computers that were in the classroom. What happened was that the students became very "fluent" in sending computer messages to each other even though they were co-present. The instructor seemed to think that this was both a wonderful idea and result. But, as Postman pointed out, the professor did miss a couple of things. "First, he was unable to get twenty human beings in a classroom to talk to each other. Moreover, the poems they were sending around all had to be read silently and thus one missed the sounds of poetry which I think most would agree is the better part of poetry."[12]

Stories like this one illustrate how our lives both inside and outside the university are being shaped to fit the technological mould of the electronic age. As Postman correctly points out, "Technopoly is a state of culture. It is also a state of mind." Later, he notes, "The computer has usurped powers and has enforced mind-sets that a fully attentive culture might have wished to deny it."[13] Given the growing interest in a technologically driven education at a distance, one well might wonder what an increasing "mechanization of the mind" might have to do with destroying the defining characteristics of higher education – namely, the curiosity and desire to engage in the critical thought of traditional scholarship. To wonder about this is to return to the social nature of knowledge production and exchange – to a sociability influenced and altered by the growth of a market-driven technology that recontextualizes and pushes us in directions heretofore unimaginable.

Certainly no one in the last thirty-some years has more carefully studied and clearly written about the effects of computer-age technology than has Sherry Turkle. In an "Author's Note: Turning Points," which serves as introductory remarks to open her book *Alone Together: Why We Expect More from Technology and Less from Each Other*, she traces the historical development of her thinking and research about computers. In a 1984 book, *The Second Self: Computers and the Human Spirit*, she asked, "How are computers changing us as people?" She didn't quite believe computer science colleagues when they answered by insisting that computers were "just tools." Her initial reservations about the "just" were strengthened when her research provided a good deal of evidence that "We are shaped by our tools. And now, the computer, a machine on the border of becoming a mind [a thinking machine], was changing and shaping us."[14]

When Turkle listened to conversations outside university seminar rooms, and to talk around kitchen tables and in children's playrooms, she discovered:

> Computers brought philosophy into everyday life: in particular, they turned children into philosophers. In the presence of their simple electronic games – games that played tic-tac-toe or challenged them in spelling – children asked if computers were alive, if they had different ways of thinking from people, and what, in the age of smart machines, was special about being a person.[15]

Because of what her research revealed, she began to see machine-human connections in a new light, focusing on computers as evocative objects capable of fostering introspection and new reflections about our developing selves.

By the time Turkle published her 1995 book *Life on the Screen: Identity in the Age of the Internet*, computer programming had combined with technological innovations to move users away from a one-on-one connection with a computer towards using it as an intermediary to help them form relationships with each other. Accordingly, she once again shifted focus as she researched this second book, which in her words "offered, on balance, a positive view of new opportunities for exploring identity online."[16] However, as her research progressed through observations of and conversations with the young "digital natives" regarding how they moved between real life (RL) and the virtual reality (VR) of the screen, her concerns grew. When connections to the internet went mobile and as robotic technology evolved, our screen machines could now travel with us, and many users saw them as potential "friends." It was all the more reason to be concerned as the fruits of robotic research "made their way into children's playrooms; by the late 1990s, children were presented with digital 'creatures' that made demands for attention and seemed to pay attention to them."[17]

Consequently, by 2011 and the last book in her technology trilogy, Turkle was focusing on yet another explicit issue. *Alone Together*, as she describes it, carries on the work of her second book, where as the result of the research, she says, "I was troubled about the costs of life with simulation." She continues:

> These days, insecure in our relationships and anxious about intimacy, we look to technology for ways to be in relationships and protect ourselves from them at the same time. . . . I feel witness for a third time to a turning point in our expectations of technology and ourselves. We bend to the inanimate with new solicitude. We fear the risks and disappointments of relationships with our fellow humans. *We expect more from technology and less from each other.*[18]

I share Turkle's concerns. The anxiousness she studies and describes is still with us some sixty-five years after David Riesman, Reuel Denney, and Nathan Glazer discussed mid-twentieth-century anxiety in their best-selling classic *The Lonely Crowd: A Study of the Changing American Character*. These authors argued that individual character and behaviour were shaped and directed by different feelings and emotions related to differing cultural orientations prominent in each case – tradition-directed (shame), inner-directed (guilt), and other-directed (anxiety). They paid special attention to other-direction and the high anxiety that results when the clear signals as to how to behave and feel, formerly provided by the familiar customs of tradition and the normative moral certainty of direction from within, lose their guiding authority. By 1950 other-direction had taken hold and anxious concerns about acceptance in ambiguous and new social situations had become commonplace, part of a daily routine heavily freighted with symbolism.[19]

But the connection between anxiety and loneliness explored by these authors is significantly different from the anxiousness that Turkle is witnessing, because they were describing relationships developed with other humans – and not connections with machines. Put simply: in the 1950s, unlike today, there was no default machine, no go-to mechanization, as powerful as the computer that would solve (and potentially help create) the problem of loneliness. Concern over anxiety fallout remains, but *Alone Together* and *The Lonely Crowd* represent quite different points on a timeline of the development of technology and the manner in which we adjust and incorporate it in daily living.

There is a somewhat frantic search for conformity suggested by other-directedness, and a worrisome dialectic encompassing and encouraging being unique or special as part of it.[20] Today, when we are increasingly directed by technology, our fascination with computers and other electronic innovations can transform our larger cultural identities, strengthening the branding and holding power of corporate capitalism. Colleges and universities, with their edubusiness-edutainment focus grounded on high-tech learning, have been significantly altered, for the worse. Higher education is heavily complicit in its own undoing, undermining its important traditional role as potential critic of the main drift. And, in the end, technology alone is not the answer.

Other educators concur on this line of thought. An *Inside Higher Ed* survey, "Partial Credit: The 2015 Survey of Faculty Attitudes on Technology," reveals that college and university faculty members in the United States remain sceptical about the benefits of online instruction. As the report notes:

> One of the largest ed-tech investments for many colleges – online courses – continues to be one of the most divisive. Only 17 percent of faculty members say for-credit online courses taught at any institution can achieve outcomes that are at least equivalent to those of in-person courses, while 53 percent disagree or strongly disagree. Faculty members are even more negative about online versions of courses they teach themselves, with 59 percent hypothesizing that an online course couldn't match the quality of face-to-face instruction.

True, ego and the self-interest of job protection might come into play in some of those responses, helping to explain how "No more than one in 10 faculty members say online courses are better than in-person courses when it comes to delivering course content, reaching at-risk and exceptional students, and interacting with students in and outside of class, among other factors." There is a divide between faculty and administrators: "Faculty members are more likely to say online courses provide the same or lower quality in these areas; administrators, the same or higher."

This gap between administrators and faculty regarding the efficacy of online vs. face-to-face in-person instruction narrows when we move from the set of mixed survey results about student achievement in each case to the question of willingness to spend money on high-tech education. Both administrators and teaching faculty seem to agree that such spending is a good investment, as a full "63 percent of faculty members and 84 percent of administrators surveyed say the portion of their institutions' budgets that has gone toward ed tech is money well spent."[21]

This part of the survey results might be interpreted as "edutainment sells" in a learning environment in which edubusiness rules. It may well be another case of self-interest with regard to faculty members' desire both to please and possibly to move away from and out of the classroom. If they are successful in putting some distance between themselves and the classroom, faculty can create a measure of freedom to move more centrally into a research role and/or along the administrative track and up the social mobility ladder of the institution that employs them. It could just be that some professors keep an administrator's disciplined and disciplining baton hiding in their back pockets.

Clifford Stoll, in sharing his second thoughts about the information highway, had it right more than twenty years ago: "I guess what I am trying to say is this: students deserve personal contact with instructors – interactive videos and remote broadcasts are no substitute for studying under a fired-up teacher who's there in person."[22] As creators of technology we have to take a reflective step back and understand that an increased reliance on our machines may not be the best and/or only answer when it comes to fulfilling our social and learning needs as humans. Turkle has cogently argued that our movement towards being alone together constitutes a "robotic moment," and that moment is about "how we are changed as technology offers us substitutes for connecting with each other face-to-face." She charts our movement from the 1980s – when in learning how to live with the computer technology that we created, "it was enough to change the way you saw yourself" – to the present moment, where "it is a question of how you live your life."

In her concern, which starts on an individual level with loneliness as "failed solitude" replaced by machines, Turkle is aware of the consequences for the collective and the culture at large. While my own concern starts at the institutional level, I share her concern that "the simplification and reduction of relationship is no longer something to [simply] complain about." The robotic moment is much more complex and complicated because "it may become what we expect, even desire."[23]

MOOC Versus Seminar

While change in how our institutions of higher learning operate is well past due, the change from in-person classroom settings to the popular high-tech MOOCs is not the fix I have in mind. Rather, I side with Carlos Spoerhase, who has elaborated upon David Bromwich's view that MOOCs are founded upon a very specific (I would add wrong-headed) idea of what constitutes an intellectual community: "At the heart of the MOOC model is the idea that education is a mediated but unsocial activity. This is as strange as the idea – shared by ecstatic communities of faith – that the discovery of truth is a social but unmediated activity."[24] Spoerhase calls to our attention an alternative model of higher education, one that is both a *mediated* and a *social* activity. This model dates back at least to the late Enlightenment and features the academic seminar. The seminar took over from and was an improvement upon the lecture, stimulating students to undertake "self-guided" inquisitive learning.

The seminar model was established as an institution, a government-approved "constituent part" of the Prussian education system in September 1787. The seminar on classical philology was taught at the University of Halle by Friedrich August Wolf, who was able to sustain his program model for the next nineteen years. There is no denying that the seminar was an elite program, with only twelve or so students chosen each year. Their admittance freed them from routinely attending lectures, and it was assumed that their seminar essays would serve to stimulate further independent inquiry and oral debate. This practice contrasts sharply with today's schooling, where such essays most often simply serve as evaluation pieces produced to earn course-assessment marks.

Spoerhase's excellent review of the seminar model as mediated social activity can be summarized with selected excerpts from his lively description:

> At the beginning of the nineteenth century, the term 'seminar' denoted a complex institution, a space that made the union of teaching and research possible. . . . It was a specific location, a meeting room, which later frequently also housed a library with study materials and accommodation. . . . They [the seminar members] schooled themselves in philological and historical methods, composed written seminar papers and, ultimately, came to model their own behaviour on the example of their director. . . . The core concept of the seminar is that a good teacher must also be a researcher.[25]

Spoerhase continues by noting that seminar meetings were generally public and well attended. Community members from outside the university were invited in. In essence they were encouraged to function as non-university-based peer reviewers who shared the student participants' quest for enlightenment and the pursuit of knowledge for its own sake, "free from the inhibiting cost-benefit calculation of everyday life."[26]

Some of Wolf's principles have been carried forward into present-day seminars, which still often emphasize interpretation and what is referred to as critical thinking, which should inform essay construction and oral debate. However, unlike most modern seminars where we depend on the professor as leader and authority figure in the classroom, offering authoritative final suggestions and critical corrections to student work, seminar director Wolf provided wide latitude by encouraging students to share in these scholarly tasks. Spoerhase's examination of the seminar papers in Wolf's literary estate reveals, "The students were also supposed to learn to appraise each other. Student criticism was an established exercise not only in the familiar form of oral debate, but also in relation to drafts of written work."[27]

What Spoerhase describes as "a web of reciprocal intellectual commitment and personal trust [that] was spun within the [Wolf] seminar" offers a sharp contrast when compared to today's MOOCs. Besides the offline-online difference made possible by high-tech education, the two models are in significant ways totally different.

> The seminar was not "massive," because it always encompassed only a small group of people. It was not "open," because participants had to meet high intellectual standards in order to be accepted. And, above all, it was not a "course," but rather a group in which the student would undertake intensive collaborative research for a period of two or three years.[28]

The traditional university of Wolf's time was predicated on the physical presence of the participants, whereas in the edubusiness university powered by high-tech electronic-based learning of the MOOCs' variety, the importance of physical presence is no longer paramount or clear. While MOOCs offer nearly unlimited opportunities to cut staff, with professors not required to be on-site, they also violate one of Wolf's most fundamental principles of seminar participation: the centrality and importance of personal conversation. Spoerhase elaborates:

His past seminarians, writing their memoirs, laid particular emphasis on this. It was an integral aspect of the educational experience that Wolf would visit the seminar participants, go for a walk with them or even join them in evening "symposia." Specialist interests were closely interwoven with personal contact in day-to-day life. Significantly, Wolf refused to be paid in the usual way for the 'private' tutoring of students, affirming that the relationship between professor and seminarians was collegial.[29]

The seminar model, then, as Wolf conceived and practised it, assured that successful learning values the process of establishing and nurturing a close community of learners just as much as any scholarly content that might be imparted. Part of discovering and being actively involved in an intellectual community rests on developing the ability to nurture conversation. Turkle is concerned, as I am, about a seemingly diminished ability in our electronic culture to rescue conversation from technology.

SEVEN

Classroom Practice and Student-Friendly Suggestions

Up Close and Personal

"**D**on't let school get in the way of your education." This admonition first appeared some twenty years ago, etched onto the wall of a bathroom stall in the men's room near my office. In a déjà vu moment it recently reappeared in slightly altered and elaborated form to include the phrase "don't let the bastards grind you down" – clearly the work of a latter-day philosopher and pundit. Given the kind of scholarly atmosphere being created in today's universities, there is a very good chance that few will be able to prevent the first phrase from becoming reality and that many will feel the weight of the second.

Certainly, one of the things that grinds down the possibility of learning in today's version of higher education is the mindset, or mentality, that worships technology. But it is more than that: it is also a mindset that sees higher learning, through the wonders of technology, as vocational job preparation above – and to the exclusion of – all else. It is a mindset that is ascendant in a darkened, long-lasting age of neoliberalism. As noted education observer William Deresiewicz states in an essay about the setback of "Neoliberal Arts," "By and large, elite American universities no longer provide their students with a real education, one that addresses them as complete human beings rather than as future specialists." Instead, the college has "Sold Its Soul to the Market." He notes the drawing power of vocational subjects among today's student body. Of course, it is common knowledge that the percentage of English and other humanities majors has "plummeted since the 1960s," but Deresiewicz uncovers other surprising statistics. Even greater than the decline of English majors is the

60 per cent drop in those majoring in the physical sciences, such as physics, chemistry, geology, and astronomy. "As of 2013, only 1.5 per cent of students graduated with a degree in one of those subjects, and only 1.1 per cent in math. At most colleges, the lion's share of undergraduates majors in vocational fields: business, communications, education, health."[1] This vocational bent is true even in elite institutions where commercial majors such as economics, biology, engineering, and computer science are most popular.

Deresiewicz describes how technology has commandeered the driver's seat both within and outside the university's ivy-covered walls:

> It is not the humanities per se that are under attack. It is learning: learning for its own sake, ideas for their own sake. It is the liberal arts, but understood in their true meaning, as all of those fields in which knowledge is pursued as an end in itself, the sciences and social sciences included. History, sociology, and political-science majors endure the same kind of ritual hazing ("Oh, so you decided to go for the big bucks") as do people who major in French or philosophy. Governor Rick Scott of Florida has singled out anthropology majors as something his state does not need more of. Everybody talks about the STEM fields – science, technology, engineering, and math – but no one's really interested in science, and no one's really interested in math: interested in funding them, interested in having their kids or their constituents pursue careers in them. That leaves technology and engineering, which means (since the second is a subset of the first) it leaves technology.[2]

For Deresiewicz, neoliberalism ("an ideology that reduces all values to money values") is everywhere, a political approach fully confident in a taken-for-granted assumption that all higher education participants and the economy as a whole will benefit by following its directions and commands for skill-set training useful in the workplace. Training for jobs becomes the centrepiece of a university education. This focus bolsters Governor Scott's proposal that would see liberal arts majors charged higher tuition at the state universities – it permits it to be taken seriously rather than seen as a badly crafted joke. It is a focus that sees higher learning as vocational job preparation, devaluing the role of considered reflection and analytical thinking that leads to the construction of cogent arguments in a learning environment in which knowledge is pursued for its own sake.

In general the university's current malaise owes much, if not everything, to this emphasis on the bottom line – on the primacy of vocational training in combination with elements such as an increasingly predatory education at a distance. Yet it remains quite possible to at least mitigate – and possibly even, in the long term, rectify – the worst aspects of these developments by focusing our energies on restoring the higher learning in universities to its original Latin term – *universitas*, meaning a community of the whole (all of us) focused on what unites us universally. This restoration would necessarily see high-tech education take a back seat to an in-person and personal approach to higher learning – a learning that accords with a firm belief in the creation and exchange of knowledge as being, above all, a social activity.

Here I offer a few suggestions for ways of moving towards this more optimistic and hopeful vision for the university, fully recognizing that at this juncture we are not readily able to tear down what has already been done in the construction of a corporate university or avoid the head-long rush towards high-tech higher learning. Specifically, my suggestions are aimed at creatively organizing classroom experiences, especially so-called "curriculum content" and learning "assignments and evaluations," in a manner that will emphasize "the social" and put a measure of both "community" and "personal attachment" back into an in-person classroom experience. My suggestions might even help all participants to reconnect with each other and begin reintegrating emotional feeling and logical rationality in such a way as to re-energize the classroom environment in the service of scholarship.

My suggestions, taken together, have in common an emphasis upon 'higher education as an open-ended exploratory process, what the Brazilian educator Paulo Freire called a "problem-solving" as opposed to a "banking" (education-as-finished-product) model.[3] My goal is to help organize classroom environments and courses in such a way that they give primacy to analytical exchange and discussion grounded upon continual reflection. For me, formal education should be part of a continuing learning experience that leads both students and professors towards knowledge-seeking, a dialectical process of analysis, reflection, re-analysis, and further reflection, which constitutes a way of being in the world long after the "pomp and circumstance" of graduation have faded. It values a higher learning that connects us as societal actors with agency to the larger social structure in a manner that, to borrow a phrase from activists in feminist movements, engages us in making "the personal political and the political personal." My suggestions are meant to encourage the imagining of alternatives to the prevailing market framework of neoliberalism with its meaninglessly ambiguous buzz words of leadership, service, and creativity (terms all noted in the Deresiewicz criticism), and its "static" reliance on technological change that does not fundamentally alter status quo arrangements. As Deresiewicz notes, "The biggest challenges we face – climate change, resource depletion, the disappearance of work in the face of automation – will require nothing less than fundamental change, a new organization of society. If there was ever a time that we needed young people to imagine a different world, that time is now."[4]

Imagining a different world can start with students and faculty working together to create a different kind of classroom experience – one that de-emphasizes an authority structure centred on the professor in favour of less highly structured and more user-friendly arrangements. After all, it is people themselves – rather than course subjects or the provision of information – who are central in creating educational experiences of long-term value. The interaction with and among people and what they stand for is the higher learning "takeaway" of value in helping students develop a sense of themselves and who they are – and in so doing, the roles they might play in reimagining a world that we too often take for granted as unchangeable.

Here again, the thought of James Farrell is instructive. Happiness as opposed to fun is not so grounded in the momentary, and, importantly, is centred more on the collective than on the individual. Farrell, speaking of happiness as fulfilment, reminds us that it does not have to be episodic, as fun often is, "nor is it necessarily fun." Fulfilment most often bypasses consumer culture in that it involves "going deep instead of skimming the surface of life. . . . So the funny thing about fun morality is how much it keeps us distracted from other possibilities of deeper pleasure."[5] But partying can have a place in helping create and develop an interest in the collectivity that reaches beyond individualized and fleeting pleasures. For, as Farrell recognizes: "The problem with fun, then, isn't its pleasure or gratification. It's that we can come to be *fun*damentally different people when we focus mainly on fun, and when we forget the quest for more substantial sources of happiness."[6]

At work are party processes that may develop new friendships and deepen old ones, build trust, and in general build social capital of value in other contexts. This is most important in understanding my suggestions aimed at transforming university classrooms. All of us who are interested in the university as an important and sustainable societal institution must somehow figure out ways of transferring weekend party capital to the

Monday morning classroom – which I believe can best be done by slowing down and lessening the grip of the pervasive (and persuasive) distractions that account for the edutainment-edubusiness culture. The party mix of spontaneity and exuberance is instructive and can be of value in the classroom, where there is great potential for drawing out and mixing emotionality and rationality. After all, emotions lie beneath the surface of rational thought. Classroom reform aimed at breaking down and resisting the false dichotomy between rationality and emotionality can offer constructive encouragement and instruction in how to bring these values together. We need to work together to remake classrooms and the university, to imagine alternatives that will serve both the best interests of students and faculty as well as the wider community outside the university.

Creating a User-Friendly Classroom: Four Experiments

For me, based on a half-century of university teaching experience, it is all about starting in the classroom – and in particular about creating user-friendly classrooms and de-emphasizing high-tech learning. While this might seem obvious enough, it is a reversal of contemporary practice: well-documented research studies have found that professors and the universities that employ them have historically placed student wishes and needs near the bottom of their hierarchy of concerns,[7] taking every opportunity to insulate themselves and their elite position from the "unwashed" (read uncertified) masses that make up the student body. Beginning in the early 1990s more attention began to be paid to the concerns of students, or more precisely the role they play as fee-paying consumers, with urgent calls to initiate university teaching reforms that would put more energy and resources into redressing the historic imbalance that emphasizes and privileges research over teaching.[8] A problem in this approach is, as one student author, Nikhil Goyal, put it, that "one size does not fit all." University teaching calls out for a re-evaluation and a re-energizing.[9]

Starting at the classroom level is admittedly somewhat of a patchwork remedy that falls far short of the revolution called for in Goyal's manifesto. Nevertheless, work on that level can help, I hope, to stimulate a return to an education as described by historian David Noble – as an ongoing process of awareness founded upon increasing individual and collective self-knowledge. In so doing, I want to make us all more aware of an important parenthetical observation that Noble offered when delineating his distinction between training and education:

(Whenever people recall their educational experiences they tend to remember above all not courses or subjects or the information imparted but people, people who changed their minds or their lives, people who made a difference in their developing sense of themselves. It is a sign of our current confusion about education that we must be reminded of this obvious fact: that the relationship between people is central to the educational experience.)[10]

These relationships between people constitute the heart and soul of what we are doing as university instructors. It is these relationships that must be remembered and re-energized if we are to succeed in transforming learning experiences for both our young people and ourselves.

With this in mind, as my suggestions for change I want to outline a number of "experiments" that I have taken in my own years of teaching: creating a less structured classroom; connecting the classroom with the surrounding community; encouraging volunteerism; and using storytelling as a key mode of learning. These experiments have a number of things in common.

1. Fundamentally and perhaps most obviously, they all transform the learning environment, the social context of the university classroom.
2. In all cases students are newly empowered, with professors relinquishing some professional authority (of office) in favour of encouraging the amateurism of students as they begin to take greater control of their classroom learning.
3. In each case this is initiated by professors modeling and encouraging students to use their personal life experiences to explore the subject matter of the course. (Admittedly this is a task and outcome more easily accomplished in the social sciences and humanities than in the so-called "natural" sciences.)
4. This emphasis on life experiences results in all cases in an opportunity for individual reflection and self-transformative growth but also, and just as important, a related opportunity to bring the wider community into the university classroom. Here there is potential for unifying what is often referred to as an alienating split between "town" and "gown" or the "real world" and the "ivory tower."
5. In each experiment a healthy sustaining diversity is served, and the debilitating effects of a "one size fits all" training monoculture grounded on professional ideology are limited.[11]

The Less-Structured Classroom

My first attempt to make the university classroom more user-friendly occurred early in my teaching career when I saw an opportunity to do something different in a third-year sociology of education evening course that was scheduled to meet in three-hour sessions once a week.[12] As a questionnaire administered on the last night of class confirmed, the relatively small number (twenty-three) who attended the first session were a diverse group of mature (average age just under thirty years) students, most of whom were employed in either full-time or part-time day jobs. My plan was to encourage a seminar-type, give-and-take experience in a less-structured classroom context, a learning environment in which the teacher, acting more as facilitator than instructor, becomes a "student" and the students become "teachers" in the fullest and best sense of these terms.

On the evening before the first class met, I had spoken with an adult educator friend who, in a recorded conversation, asked me some pointed questions centred upon difficulties and consequences connected with relinquishing a measure of classroom power as an authority figure and what might be required in the way of scholarly preparation and organization. What did I have in mind regarding my role in the creation of this different kind of learning environment? The following evening, at the first meeting of the class, I briefly answered this question for the students, suggesting that it would take the remainder of the course and beyond to offer a more complete answer. I told them about my research interests and teaching background in the sociology of education and what I did *not* have for them – a course outline to be covered, required texts to be read, among other things. I offered a succinct and carefully prepared statement: "For the record, I would rather not run this as a traditional course. I'd like to help make this course a 'happening.' In other words, I'd like this course to become what we as a group want it to become. I would prefer that this course be as much 'an open book' to begin with as possible." I elaborated, voicing the hope that the group as a whole would construct a process-oriented, always provisional "learning agenda" together, and that this would lead to readings and discussions centred upon shared problems and issues. I finished with these pointed sentences: "As far as I am concerned it's open. There is an unwritten agenda here to be filled in."[13]

The rest of that first evening was spent in animated discussion. We introduced ourselves to one another and talked about potential learning projects, what we might do at next week's class session and for the remainder of the year. We discussed the matter of evaluation as well, but the usual concern with marks or grades was not a focal point. The fear that comes with moving away from a teacher-centred classroom diminished as we began to acclimate ourselves to the exciting prospect of trying to create something new together. Something akin to fear, certainly a large helping of uncertainty, peaked for me when, thirty minutes into the course, two students got up and walked out. They left the distinct impression that this attempt to create a new learning environment was an unexpected surprise that was not for them. I immediately shared my reaction to this rather abrupt student departure with the remaining students. I spoke about the emotions I was feeling with regard to my confidence in relation to teaching, my ego involvement as a teacher, and the leap of faith required for both myself and the students as we let this classroom process of change unfold.

This kind of talk about personal involvement and our growing self-knowledge and emotional investment in our learning gradually became commonplace in our differently structured classroom. It was just this kind of openness that permitted us to overcome some of the most debilitating effects of the ever-present hidden curriculum of cultural capital biases and inequities resting upon background differences with regard to social class, race-ethnicity, and gender.

For example, discussion contributions from the few class members, predominantly women, from working-class families were able to give the other 80 per cent of us with middle- or upper-middle-class backgrounds a better understanding of, a reflective pause concerning, these women's struggles to attain, and the pride they felt in obtaining, a university education. All class members benefited as two women told their stories of being raised in "union families" by parents active in promoting the rights of workers. All of us were compelled to rethink not only the important role that immigrants played in building Canada but also commonly held views such as the one that views unions as socialist-tinged organizations that have outlived their usefulness. A Québécois woman and a First Nations woman with a background that included extensive experience as a client of the welfare system struggled to explain their ethnic and cultural differences to the rest of us (with our English, English-Canadian, and American ancestry). As in the stories of social class, their success in doing so – in explaining the contributions of their people in creating the modern Canadian mosaic – benefited everyone, helping us all to better understand and bridge race-ethnic differences.

The less-structured classroom, in revealing and countering the hidden curriculum, also had an effect with regard to gender. The usual gender split, often discussed in sociological literature, underscores a reality emphasizing that men are more "instrumental" and less "expressive" in their view of the world than are women. The answers to my end-of-course questionnaire indicated that our less-structured student-centred classroom environment tended to even things out in this regard, with the men in particular feeling more comfortable in expressing their feelings and emotions in front of class members. Possibly this was because we had become somewhat "known" to each other, encouraging each other not to be afraid of our diversities and instead to recognize, confront, and express our feelings about difference. We developed a sense of knowing each other as "real people" – what Noble talked about as "individual and collective self-knowledge," and Abraham Maslow infamously referred to as "self-actualization."[14] Our classroom interaction was vitally and positively altered, as I noted at the time: "In short, there was a tie between us, a sense of relationship among us, not often found in other more highly-structured and traditional courses, that made this class special for *everyone*, including myself."[15]

The personal disclosures and the self-growth, light-bulb-over-head clicks of recognition and new awareness did take some getting used to, but so too did the laughter and noise level in our transformed classroom setting. At least twice during the first semester our learning became so physically active and so much fun that the atmosphere forced us, rather self-consciously, to close the doors. In one session, under a student's direction, we practised the co-ordination of body and mind through creative movement. This boisterous exercise in building an awareness of self and others, in encouraging feelings of self-worth, and developing both movement and creative-thinking skills brought students on break from other classes to the hallway doors and windows of our classroom to see what was happening and join in the fun of learning. We got a similar response with another exercise, when we divided into small groups and attempted to make the largest bubble possible with plastic straws, string, soap, water, and buckets. After brainstorming different ways of accomplishing the task, each of us had to learn how to work with others, to use past experience to implement new ideas. What we took away from this exercise was a lesson in how co-operative learning can enhance and trump individual learning.

This unusual classroom learning atmosphere of a group-organized and directed curriculum not only made collective use of the combined resources and experience of everyone in the seminar but also informed the personalized learning agendas on display in the students' (and the instructor's) year-long projects. These did not constitute a "culminating activity" (a phrase used by many of today's education professors in reference to an end-of-term production of a learned commodity). Rather, the great majority of our projects constituted not a finished product but a continuum of learning and self-development that went on well after classroom sessions ended in April.

The best projects we undertook showcased this process. One of them involved a government employee who was moved by a class discussion and some readings on adult education and retraining to attempt to come to grips with his strong feelings concerning the inadequacy of the training programs he was administering in his job at Canada Employment and Immigration. He believed the programs were largely a waste of taxpayers' money and that they were preventing him from doing his job properly. In gathering supportive evidence from his work experience and researching why and how various non-governmental agencies had become involved with government-initiated training, he began to draw a clear and refined picture of the situation that he was confronting every day at work. This new understanding both lessened his frustration and served as a springboard to thoughts about alternative procedures and policies that might make the training programs more effective for his clients.

In another case one of our students, a mother on leave from her profession, was working at home taking care of her two young children. After a couple of class discussions and readings about the common practice of drugging "hyperactive" children into submission simply so they can get through their school days, she told us her story. She was experiencing intense frustration on a daily basis. One of her children was exhibiting what she referred to as "severe behaviour problems" and experiencing extreme difficulties both at school and at home. The discussion, and the class reading, led to a project: she began to keep a close and detailed record of her child's behaviour; during the course of the school year she gained the knowledge and confidence to make significant changes in the child's diet and to start using megavitamin and naturopathic therapy in place of Ritalin and other amphetamines ("speed"), all the while keeping a detailed record of the effects of these changes. In the end she was able to help her child make necessary and healthy adjustments that both bettered the situation at school and considerably reduced tensions – and, consequently, her level of frustration – among family members at home; but in the process she and our whole class came to a broader sociological understanding regarding the appropriateness (the "normalness") of some responses of hyperactive students to the many intolerable situations that the institution of formal schooling creates for all children.[16]

These two projects and others that came out of this experiment in creating a less-structured classroom benefited all course members. The course helped us all to build greater individual and community awareness, a self-knowledge necessary to overcome the limits of "business-as-usual" thinking dominated by taken-for-granted polarizations that separate learning from content, theory from practice, and political from personal matters. In essence this course encouraged the growth of Mills's "sociological imagination," providing excellent examples of that creative intersection where individual biography meets institutional social structure.

Community Connections and Volunteerism

This imagination was also at work in two other smaller classes, each with a dozen students. These were senior-level courses, one taught by myself and the other a collaborative effort with my daughter, Rebecca Collins-Nelsen, also a sociologist. They were organized in a slightly more-structured fashion with course outlines, somewhat provisional, and a few required specialized readings appropriate for undergraduate and graduate sociology students in their fourth and fifth years of university study. In both courses we made a conscious attempt to encourage students to engage by starting with their personal experiences and following this up by developing learning projects with the objective of bringing the community outside academia into their work.

Ties between the university classroom and the surrounding environment thus often became the focal point for student reflections upon their own experiences away from the confines of the university. Course projects reflected this emphasis. For instance, one project – a fourth-year seminar in the "Sociology of Everyday Life" – included work by two athletes who in other courses had experienced academic difficulties typified by the phrase "dumb jock." Now, to the contrary, one of them detailed how his experience as a football player was a useful bridge to the wider community, contributing to his potential as a successful candidate for a teaching career. The other shared his record of participant-observations as a player on the basketball team, which led to a discussion of sociability groups and community connections that gave us a new appreciation of the term "student-athlete" and helped to explain his career choice in becoming an RCMP officer. The oldest class member, a forty-something laid-off mill worker, examined mill and factory closures and downsizings that led us to explore both the corporate domination that structures relations between unions and management and the resulting fallout that damages personal and family relationships. Reflections by a health-care professional showed us how and why she was engaged in translating and transferring her work experience in "Third World" conditions in an African country to her work at a Frontier College–like literacy program with people in the Canadian North. Then there was the auto-ethnographic work of a former Greenpeace volunteer turned tree planter who turned her diary of summer employment in the forest industry into a reflection on her jewelry-crafting and hemp clothes-making hobbies. Her experience sparked a creative discussion regarding the potential of sustainable employment opportunities – and provided a lesson in environmental conservation of interest to all. Another student's record of volunteer work in social justice activities became the centrepiece of her exploration of the meaning, legal and otherwise, of that engagement, which informed us all as a group and gave her further impetus to continue her formal schooling and eventually find employment as a conflict-resolution mediator.

The volunteerism component of that project played a key role in a course on community and culture that my daughter and I did with graduate students. In the very first class session a majority of class members voiced their desire to make the course "more real" by bringing the surrounding community into the classroom, and vice versa. We all agreed to volunteer and keep a participant-observation record, or journal, of our experiences. Class members worked in a variety of capacities with agencies and programs: an adult literacy agency, a home for senior adults, a diversity centre that helped immigrants make the transition to their new and unfamiliar environment, an elementary-school breakfast program, the executive board of a nursery pre-school, a soup kitchen, and a church-sponsored group engaged in community social work activities. I even managed to improve my almost non-existent French by using my basketball-playing experience to land an assistant coaching position at the local francophone high school, where I became quite proficient in shouting "*avance*" and "*bouge tes pieds*."

Storytelling

Both my daughter and I found a storytelling approach to be highly effective in teaching large lecture sections of introductory sociology to several hundred first-year students.[17] Eventually, rather than adopting the norm of speaking in abstractions, we used stories of everyday interactions, several of them autobiographical, as starting points. After telling these stories we used them to tease out the introductory sociological concepts and theories that were essential elements in the courses.

One story that I have used several times draws upon events occurring in the late 1960s, when I was in my mid-twenties and holding down my first full-time job as a sociology instructor at the State University of New York Albany.[18] A former colleague who wanted to abandon his university teaching career needed to figure out a way to replace his rather handsome professor's salary. He was under intense financial pressure because in the years leading up to his decision he and his partner had fostered and adopted three hard-to-place pre-schoolers as additions to their original family of three children. The story turns on their solution, which entailed a clever adherence to and legal manipulation of bureaucratic rules at both the federal government employment office and a state-controlled county child welfare office in Albany. The employment agency sponsored the couple's strategy of shared and permanent unemployment that allowed one or the other parent on a continual basis to stay out of the paid labour force and remain at home looking after child care and family matters. The child welfare office agreed to continue providing child-subsidy payments even when this blended family decided to move all the way across the United States to settle near their childhood homes outside of Seattle, Washington. This state-to-state payment continuation with regard to child adoption subsidies was one of the first, if not the first, agreements of this kind (and it even included moving expenses).

The story raised ethical and moral questions as well as some outrage directed at "pogey" and "welfare" cheaters. As the instructor I proceeded by connecting a few dots. The partners in this particular couple, with their many years of formal schooling, had the literacy necessary to see them through the painstaking process of properly filling out bureaucratic forms. The result is that some potential clients with potentially legitimate claims on the services of a particular bureaucracy are better equipped than others to present a "normal" case, one that meets with the approval of various officials. With this explanation providing a new and different perspective for the students, the tone of our discussion changed. The story sparked further discussion, both about how schools and other bureaucracies function and about how social-class inequalities and differences in cultural capital are connectable to favourable and unfavourable outcomes for clients serviced by various bureaucratic organizations. Students joined in with bureaucratic tales drawn from their own experiences, involving everything from university registration protocol to job searches, unemployment income rules, cellphone company hassles, online dating, and more. In class, encouraged to make sociological use of their stories both in verbal exchanges and in their term papers, the students routinely presented a veritable smorgasbord of experience.

At bottom this storytelling approach, like other methods designed to alter the standard teacher-centred classroom, encouraged students to take seriously their everyday life experiences, to do the best they could to seriously reflect upon and incorporate them as part of the course material. Students were enticed and encouraged to take on, or at least partially assume, the role of non-certified experts in the subject matter at hand – to move from being professional students to amateur professors. This is a makeover that makes courses and the classroom more user-friendly and thus stimulates and facilitates a kind of learning that can be intriguing, fascinating, and fun – a renewable cycle of reinforcement that keeps on giving.

Taken together such learning "experiments" constitute a low-tech test of what social media observer Clay Shirky discusses in analyzing the effects of web-based technology.[19] He pays particular attention to how groups form and function in altering the social contexts of communication. It is an approach that, in my experience, has some potential to encourage instructors to trust in the developing abilities of students as creditable amateur observers. Shirky speaks of "mass amateurism" and contends that web-based technology creates a social context favouring sharing and a particular kind of individualism – "sharing anchors community" and "everyone is a media outlet."[20] Each individual has an important voice that should be heard, not in the service of individualism but rather, I would hope, in service to students' developing sense of the collectivity. The community that is being anchored here is a classroom group of university students who will ideally use their developing knowledge both to bring in and reach out to larger communities beyond the university. The various "experimental" approaches are something of a non-computer-based trial run of the feasibility and general value of encouraging diversity in a "Here Comes Everybody" classroom grounded upon equity and opportunity.

Indigenous Storywork: Learning about Its Potential for Transforming University Classrooms

In her important book *Indigenous Storywork: Educating the Heart, Mind, Body, and Spirit*, education professor Jo-ann Archibald expresses a desire "to find a respectful place for stories and storytelling in education, especially in curricula."[21] That desire, of course, has a strong resonance with my own emphasis on a classroom storytelling approach – although in noting the connections I, as a Caucasian of Eurocentric background, in no way mean to appropriate the distinct cultural experience of being Indigenous or Aboriginal in the United States or Canada.

Due to the many differences that separate her cultural contexts from my own, our stories and the manner in which we go about telling them are bound to be different. This is as it should be. But again, what she learned from the Elders concerning "the seven principles related to using First Nations stories and storytelling for educational purposes (respect, responsibility, reciprocity, reverence, holism, interrelatedness, and synergy")[22] – what I term storywork – has a great deal of relevance for my own approach. What she reports as the classroom experience that often results in her work with young children where "It is [as] though the story 'comes alive' and becomes the teacher,"[23] is what I hope for as a favourable outcome in my own work with older students.

My storywork pedagogy is similar to Archibald's in that it is grounded upon the idea that we can learn from listening attentively to the life experiences of others, and in turn share our own backgrounds in a manner that welcomes and learns from their interpretations. My students and I often do this around a seminar table in a classroom. Archibald points out that this is just one of several "common approaches," which include "telling stories with no explanation, using a talking circle for discussion, role playing and having fun with the stories, and story repetition."[24] Professors who (like myself) do not share similar experiences with Indigenous peoples, those of us who are part of the colonizing culture that continues to oppress them, have much to learn. As it is with Archibald's Indigenous elementary-school students, "We need to bring back storytelling in ways that respectfully and responsibly resonate with the cultural community of the students,"[25] most of whom in my case are non-indigenous. This means creating a focused space in the university classroom (Archibald calls it "zeroing in") where students and professors alike have an opportunity to engage in reflective thinking and feeling. This approach reminds us what higher education at its best should be about – learning that educates rather than simply being satisfied with skill training. One of Archibald's colleagues, Lorna Mathias, elaborated upon this insight. She was concerned about the meanings and understandings that students not familiar with an oral tradition were taking away from the stories being told: "I was reminded that the skills taught in basic reading lessons, when used in conjunction with First Nations stories, should not overpower the stories so that the skills become the important aspect of the lesson, rather than the teachings in the stories."[26]

These teachings, Indigenous and other, are ongoing, and story-telling can have a powerful role to play in understanding oppression from all sides. As Archibald points out, stories can reaffirm and strengthen cultural tradition and practices, protecting against harmful assimilation: "Indigenous peoples' history of colonization has left many of our peoples and our cultures weak and fragmented. Cultural knowl-edge, traditions, and healing have lessened the detrimental effects of colonization. Cultural knowledge and traditions have also helped us to resist assimilation."[27] From the other side of the colonization divide, many social analysts before and after Karl Marx have noted that mem-bers of the oppressing dominant culture are also alienated and oppressed by their own practices; and furthermore, that the point about oppression is not simply to study it but to change it – so that all may experience less alienation and more freedom.

The Extension of Learning "Our Own Stuff" and Beyond

The thing about storytelling and other less teacher-centred classroom options is that they all focus on working with what philosopher-mechanic Matthew B. Crawford refers to as "our own stuff." Crawford speaks of our paradoxical experience of agency in our intensely materi-alist culture, where our attempt "to be master of our own stuff entails also being mastered by it."[28] He uses the example of the relatively new "no hands" water faucets in public washrooms – faucets without a han-dle, where you wave your hand underneath to get the water flowing. It is a technology that calls on users to make an on-spot adjustment, and which carries the implicit presumption of irresponsibility. Those who have designed this and other technologies that are manually disengaged require users to jump through several mental hoops in order to be able to interpret the new gadget as being both more convenient and rational than the old. This and other so-called "improvements" seem to reveal "an ideology of freedom at the heart of consumerist material culture: a promise to disburden us of mental and bodily involvement with our own stuff so we can pursue ends we have freely chosen. Yet this disburdening gives us fewer occasions for the experience of direct responsibility."[29] What he describes is akin to the web-like treatments of learning, including distilled and posted instructor notes on course material related to lectures and readings, which absolve students of both the ability and the responsibility of producing their own material – of the opportunity to develop their own note-taking and organizational skills that might serve them well long after the course lectures are over. Unlike storytelling, the no-handle water faucet and the posted notes constitute a kind of high-tech "spoon-feeding," an infantilization, that separates us from an understanding and mastering of that which is or could be ours.

To engage with what is ours, to apply what is learned in the classroom to our lives outside school, and to bring the outside world into the classroom have never been more important than in the present moment. All of our "own stuff" – everything – is at risk now that the global economy and culture shaped by our unyielding appetite for fossil fuel have resulted in pushing us to the brink of destroying our planet. This is the message of economic critic and activist Naomi Klein, in her aptly titled *This Changes Everything*.[30] As with storytelling, we have much to learn from Indigenous peoples. We should, for instance, be paying attention to their demands for consultation when outside forces attempt to wrest from their control the land they occupy and value, as well as to their tradition of applying the wisdom of looking seven generations ahead when making decisions. Of course, if we do not change our ways quickly, we may not have seven generations left. The best climate science tells us to reorient our priorities and to radically change how we live – a message to which all of us in Canada and the United States need to pay heed.

Role models and activist leaders in Indigenous communities that are opposed to the destructive occupation of their lands by resource-extracting corporations are delivering that message. In Hamilton, where I now reside, and in the greater Toronto area, we have a good example in the protest movement against the proposed "Line 9" movement of oil – with its attempt to block a refitting plan by energy giant Enbridge Inc. to use a thirty-eight-year-old pipeline to ship ultra-heavy tar sands crude (unrefined) oil east through Canada and the United States. The line carries conventional oil across Ontario and Quebec, and even the delivery of this less heavy oil has had its "accidents" or "leaks" and continuing safety concerns. Moreover, the Enbridge application to Canada's National Energy Board not only asks to change what kind of oil would go through Line 9 but also asks to reverse the course of the line. This plan to further increase tar sand oil profits domestically and through foreign exports would endanger the safety of communities beyond the Ontario-Quebec borders as the oil moves to Montreal and then through an expected second pipeline that would carry it south to Portland, Maine, for export. A project like this calls for environmentalists to take a united stand – to bridge social class, racial and ethnic, gender, and age differences – and to follow the lead of our Indigenous peoples. As "The Leap Manifesto" puts it, "The time for energy democracy has come: wherever possible communities should collectively control new clean energy systems. Indigenous peoples and others on the front lines of industrial activity should be first to receive public support for their own clean energy projects."[31] If we act immediately, we might be able to author a story with a chance of being read and passed on seven generations from now.

Beyond the warnings from university-employed scientists, what are our colleges and universities as institutions contributing to this fight to save our planet from ruin? Unfortunately, the answer is not very much – not nearly enough. Despite a global movement to encourage fossil-fuel divestment, colleges and universities in both the United States and Canada have been slow to act. California's Stanford University has been leading the way, and its success in divesting endowment funds has been notable. The Fossil Free Stanford student organization began its strong protest efforts in November 2015 with a protest rally and march ending with a sit-in at the administrative offices of the university president, and carried this action over into 2016. This organization's sustained efforts are keeping the pressure on the university's Board of Governors to keep divesting until Stanford's investments are fossil-fuel-free.

On the other side of the country, the east coast is home to Unity College of Maine, which in 2012 became the first North American college to commit to divestment. However, America's premier and wealthiest university, Harvard, has steadily resisted the demands of several student-inspired divestment groups. The university has not altered an investment portfolio that continues to pour billions of dollars into coal, gas, and oil companies. Indeed, by January 2015, after nearly three years of agitation and confrontation calling for divestment, Harvard had increased its direct investments in fossil fuel.[32] Clearly, there is work to be done if this movement is to achieve more than symbolic importance.

As a Canadian research brief on fossil-fuel divestment at universities found: "In Canada, the divestment campaign is steadily growing across several post-secondary institutions. So far [in 2015] there are 34 active divestment groups in college campuses that are spread across nine provinces."[33] With this promising start, the support of faculty, alumni, and community members who have joined this largely student-led movement remains crucial, and pressure on university boards must be unrelenting. Concordia University in Montreal became (in November 2014) the first Canadian school to divest a portion of its endowment, but as campaign organizers were quick to point out, this partial divestment of $5 million from fossil fuels is but a small portion of the total needed.[34] At McMaster, where proximity to Line 9 should make the university an excellent and timely candidate for divestment, so far there is only talk. But McMaster is not alone in that regard: by late 2016 not one college or university in Canada had managed to fully divest in fossil fuels. Our institutions of higher learning seem to be all in it together and headed in the wrong direction. This togetherness is not comforting, only troubling.

Canadian anthropologist and ethnobotanist Wade Davis offers another perspective on these issues. In an analysis of the Royal Dutch Shell company's project to "develop" the Sacred Headwaters basin in British Columbia, he points out:

> Environmental concerns aside, think for a moment what these proposals imply about our culture. We accept it as normal that people who have never been on the land, who have no history or connection to the country, may legally secure the right to come in and by the very nature of their enterprises leave in their wake a cultural and physical landscape utterly transformed and desecrated. . . . The cost of destroying a natural asset, or its inherent worth if left intact, has no metric in the economic calculations that support the industrialization of the wild. No company has to compensate the public for what it does to the commons, the forests, mountains, and rivers, which by definition belong to everyone. . . . If you think about it, especially from the perspective of so many other cultures, touched and inspired by quite different visions of life and land, it appears to be very odd and highly anomalous human behaviour.[35]

Davis's explanation for that kind of behaviour centres on the human quest for personal freedom inspired by the Renaissance and continuing into what we refer to, perhaps mistakenly, as the Enlightenment period. Those of us who followed in this European tradition, he says, "liberated the human mind from the tyranny of absolute faith, even as we freed the individual from the collective, which was the sociological equivalent of splitting the atom. And, in doing so, we also abandoned many of our intuitions for myth, magic, mysticism, and perhaps most importantly, metaphor."[36]

For Davis, the social sciences – "an oxymoronic turn of phrase if there ever was one" – represent a dubious element in the overall triumph of science: a "triumph of secular materialism [that] became the conceit of modernity." It is a conceit that dismisses as "ridiculous" notions of a living land and the meanings that might be found in observations and spiritual beliefs connected to non-human species (as an example he uses the flight of a hawk).[37]

Davis speaks for all of us concerned about the continued fossil-fuel fixation and other abuses of our environmental stewardship when he laments the scientistic "reduction of the world to a mechanism, with nature but an obstacle to overcome, a resource to be exploited." This scientistic way of thinking "has in good measure determined the manner in which our cultural tradition has blindly interacted with the living planet." As he also argues: "It is neither change ('the one constant in history') nor technology ('All peoples in all places are always dancing with new possibilities for life') that threatens the integrity of culture. It is power, the crude face of domination." His remarks reinforce a sense of hopefulness based on the understanding that "if human beings are the agents of cultural destruction, we can also be the facilitators of cultural survival."[38] In other words, humans have the potential to turn the current university mess around, preserving the institutional positives while implementing improvements and changes that will make things better.

Ensuring that our planet survives is a mission that all of us must take on. We might take our lead from the storytelling approach, as well as other approaches that are designed to alter the standard teacher-centred classroom by encouraging all to take on and at least partially assume the role of non-certified experts in the subject matter at hand. Certainly planet sustainability is the most important matter imaginable. It is a task of protection, renewal, and regeneration that should not be left solely in the hands of certified professionals and determined business entrepreneurs. We all must put our shoulder to the wheel, for time is short and the window on environmental sustainability is quickly closing. We must focus, listen, and change in order to create a new and different narrative for the time ahead.

EIGHT

Cleaning up the Mess

Putting Students and the Larger Community First

I n the over twenty months that it has taken to write this book, little has changed. Universities continue to experience more of the same, and the mess grows day by day. Parents continue to hover and argue on their adult children's behalf as all of them become more aware of the shortcomings of today's university.

Recently, as I returned to the Lakehead campus to keep my retired hand in a teaching context, a trip to the security office to renew my parking permit resulted in the usual 2 per cent fee increase. I also found that those of us paying for parking in the "G" or General lot no longer needed to worry about whether or not the electrical plug-ins were juiced up. During the two years I had been away the plug-ins had been completely removed, leaving the naked attachment posts as a sad reminder of better, more prosperous days. The same change had occurred in the adjacent and more expensive "R" or Reserved lots.

Perhaps, I optimistically thought, the great plug-in removal represented a concession to and a heightened awareness of climate change. However, if this was a "green revolution" featuring reduction in energy use and possibly even fossil-fuel divestment, it did not extend to R Lot no. 5, the parking spaces close by the central administration building. Here the plug-ins regularly supplied with the cold-weather starting balm of electricity remained. I discovered that this lot not only had a "Wait List" but also had a wait list for the "Wait List," neither of which applied to the easy access enjoyed by those in the upper reaches of the university hierarchy. The list manoeuvring and jostling that would-be vehicle parkers often carried on over a six-year period before achieving success did not include students, whose competition was not welcome: they were prohibited from parking their vehicles in this favoured lot. Certainly the unwashed (read uncertified) should learn to know their place and needn't bother trying to mix with their betters. Status and prestige carried the day, and the only green had nothing to do with environmental awareness but more likely something to do with jealousy, envy, and the bottom line. To borrow from novelist Kurt Vonnegut, "So it goes."[1]

If the edubusiness model governs parking-lot renovations, what goes on in the classroom? The emphasis on what is often narrow job training and the online MOOCs course experience grows, while the more personalized attention of the in-person classroom experience recedes along with the scholarly orientation often associated with the traditional bricks and mortar university. The professionalism and skills training that support and maintain status quo arrangements are passed from faculty bureaucrats to their student acolytes, many of whom continue to turn their creative energies towards gaming the system.

Student cheating scandals still plague university faculty and administrators, with a variety of incidents reported across the United States (colleague reports from where I teach and from afar indicate that Canada is not immune). A 2016 incident occurred at the football powerhouse and noted party school Ohio State University, with its reigning national champion Buckeyes. Students, eighty-five of them in the veterinary medicine college, were called out for allegedly sharing answers in online take-home exams for which group work was not permitted.[2] So it goes, and Party On! Pet owners might well be advised to carefully scrutinize where they take Rover and Felix the next time the animals are in need of medical care.

With professors jealously continuing to protect the boundaries of their traditional academic disciplines, professionalism is alive. But early reports suggest welcome news related to university structural change, although perhaps not so welcome to professors with regard to the discipline turf wars of boundary maintenance and the pursuit of specialized research interests and funding – a pursuit often indulged in at the expense of the quality of students' classroom experience and growth as scholars. The restructuring news comes out of Plymouth State University in New Hampshire. On June 20, 2016, that institution announced "an aggressive set of changes to its organizational structure." The plan is to scrap its current twenty-four academic departments and replace them with seven academic clusters: arts and technology; education, democracy, and social change; exploration and discovery; health and human enrichment; innovation and entrepreneurship; justice and security; and training, environment, and sustainable development. The university will still award traditional degrees, but now, in addition, "students will be able to earn certificates in specialty areas within clusters." This massive, perhaps unprecedented, structural change will be painful, with "voluntary" retirements and "separation" leavings under duress, other staff lay-offs, and several dozen positions cut and not refilled.[3] Given the individual and community pain resulting from such damaging cutbacks, I shall forego saying the usual, "So it goes."

On a brighter economic note, at least from the administration's point of view, the hope is that this wholesale change under the cluster model will not only pass muster when it comes to accreditation reviews but also, by reducing the usual or traditional institutional tinkering with bureaucratic layering, make university operations more efficient. The edubusiness hope is, of course, dollar-driven. President Donald Brix, the architect of this overhaul, argues that the reorganization and resultant cut in expenditures will make Plymouth State more competitive – in his words, help it "to get ahead of the wave." It will thus be more likely to survive in a tough market. He believes his new-look university will be instrumental not only in increasing his school's enrollment but also in retaining students once they are enrolled.[4] Here I can say, "So it goes."

This experiment at Plymouth appears to be moving beyond the recent trendy fascination of interdisciplinary programs that only minimally alter the traditional boundaries imposed by the academic department model. My hope for it is somewhat different in kind than President Brix's vision. My point of view, in keeping with the arguments expressed throughout this book, supports his vision that the reorganization may make the university more responsive to innovation. As well, and most importantly, this new structure might open up proprietary laboratory and research secrets and the university as a whole to partnerships with the local community that are not primarily driven by the profit motive. I see the potential in this restructuring – but only if the outcomes emphasize and strongly support a fundamental change away from edubusiness capitalism, where knowledge is socially produced but privately expropriated. I want the taxpayers to be served – with the health and well-being of the general public as the number one priority and beneficiary. There should be no more outcomes in which the main focus is to further line the already deep pockets of greedy capitalists and their monopolistic corporations. For me, the next five to ten years will show whether the Plymouth experiment is a dream come true or more of the same old nightmarish mess.

Meanwhile at Plymouth State and all across the United States, Canada, and elsewhere, wealthy capitalists continue to use and abuse colleges and universities, moulding them to their own purposes. Individual and corporate "benefactors," in the manner of Charles Koch, compete to have their names and economic-political philosophies immortalized by sponsoring the construction of buildings, institutes, schools, research laboratories, and chairs. In 2016 Jack Stripling provided an update and more detail on how George Mason University became Koch's "academic darling."[5] Similarly, Matthew Barakat provides interesting details of the school's growth since its founding in 1972, indicating how it parallels Koch's growing philanthropy. Koch serves as benefactor of many U.S. universities, and many commentators – going beyond the well-documented push he gets for his market-dictated libertarian ideological and political agenda – suspect that there are strings attached to his gifts. School administrators and board members have rebuffed the several attempts by George Mason's faculty senate to get details on the growing number of grant agreements between the Koch Foundation and the school. Quite possibly these agreements do not in any way restrict academic freedom, but without access to the exact wording of the agreement, who knows? The school's long-standing relationship with Koch and his money might make overt restrictions mostly unnecessary, and it seems reasonable to think that the nearly $48 million that the Foundation gave the university between 2011 and 2014 might buy silence.[6] That kind of silence and the sheer difficulties of prying loose agreement details have much to do with the growth of university bureaucracies that are top heavy with administrators charged with the duty of soliciting funds from corporate and individual benefactors. These are the same benefactors who dominate university governing boards and whose fiscal authority over budgets makes a mockery of the supposed bicameral structure that features the faculty senate on the academic side. In the ascent of the edubusiness university, money talks and academic bullshit walks as big money continues to block faculty attempts to maintain even a modicum of control over academic matters. The stage is set for both vocationalism and edutainment.

University bureaucracies continue to increase at what seems like an almost exponential rate. Pompous vice-presidents, deans, directors, and assorted other administrators regularly attend paid-for lunches, dinners, and out-of-town professional development conferences. They get uncounted weeks of paid holiday time each year. Someone has to mind the shop while they are off galavanting, and that task falls to the university support staff, their underlings at the bottom end of the edubusiness hierarchy. Secretaries and administrative assistants (some without union protection) work under constant anxiety-producing pressure to keep track of forms and meet bureaucratic deadlines. Most of them are not fooled by the change in office nomenclature from "Personnel" to "Human Resources," for as workers of the underclass they recognize that they are routinely treated more like objects than people. They are not only underappreciated, but in my experience too often abused. They do this "grunt" work for make-ends-meet salaries that amount to somewhere around 30 per cent of what their professor bosses make.

The money squeezed from shortchanging employees and solicited from well-off alumni is not often invested in academic programs and the classroom. Rather, in today's university it is most often used to create an ever-growing number of administrative offices and missions. One of the most important of these at Lakehead carries the name, "Office of Institutional Planning and Analysis." The appellation not only serves as a description of how it is supposed to function, but also embodies the edubusiness of today's higher education – the "Branding and Marketing" (the name chosen by Lakehead for its important division or department that handles these matters).

At the centre of branding and marketing is edutainment. Saturday afternoons and evenings are spent indulging in higher education's modern version of bread and circuses. Fans in the hundreds of thousands flock to massive football stadiums and basketball arenas to cheer on their school gladiators. The parties that accompany these festivals have become legion. Well-heeled alumni eagerly and aggressively line up to emulate Nike's and Oregon's Phil Knight and other philanthropists successful in turning edutainment into big money profits. The mass media provide thorough coverage of the sporting exploits of the alma mater, which in turn offer unprecedented opportunities to market every good and service imaginable. The party atmosphere of the game-day tailgate stokes the profitable fires of an edubusiness edutainment that has moved from the gridiron and the hardwood to the classroom. So it goes, and Party On!

Still, at least a slight movement away from this trend may be in the offing as less prominent and successful schools in the college sports industry begin to reconsider their ride on the edutainment sports band-wagon. In June 2016 the University of Idaho announced its decision to drop out of the NCAA's Football Bowl Subdivision (FBS) and return to playing in the less prestigious Football Championship Subdivision (FCS). Most schools, as Idaho did, struggle to reach the high status of the FBS and to attain the prestige that goes with playing at this top level. Most are not likely to reverse their course to play in the less prestigious FCS. University president Chuck Staben put Idaho's decision into an academic context: "What attracts students to our institution is the quality of academic programs, the great outcomes and the preparation for life after college. It's a great research institution. Football and athletics just complement that. We're choosing to ensure that students can compete on the field and get a great education." Of course, this is what Staben is supposed to say as the leader of an institution of higher learning. In the face of considerable alumni concern and disapproval regarding the decision, the president might have added some important economic figures to his remarks. As journalist Jake New notes: "Idaho has the lowest revenue in the FBS and its football team plays in the division's smallest stadium, an enclosed concrete structure that seats 16,000."[7]

Idaho's issues with the failure to profit on football are not the whole story, and the Vandals are not alone in suffering sports-related economic woes. An NCAA study of athletic department budgets in 2013 found that expenses outpaced or exceeded revenue in all but 20 of 128 FBS schools, with the average loss among the Power 5 conferences being $2.3 million. Interestingly, among the FCS schools, the group Idaho is set to join, the economics are reversed, with revenues since 2012 showing an increase over expenses of slightly more than 2 per cent. In the small-school Division II and III levels, revenues failed to exceed expenses in every case.[8] But that's okay: while those schools spend relatively little on athletics, in the powerhouse schools the branding factor and value of sports advertising make the losses acceptable. Idaho's Staben, going off script from his academic defence of the university, indicated the importance of brand advertising and its connection to sports success, admitting that being unable to compete successfully in football has damaged his university's brand.[9]

Despite the case of Idaho and other schools following its lead in reconsidering university athletics, the winning combination of edutainment and edubusiness will almost certainly continue to dominate for the foreseeable future. There are several groups of participants in higher learning that have been severely disadvantaged as this combination has developed. One such group is the growing legion of Ph.D.-certified university instructors who, considering the steep and continuing decline in renewal and creation of tenure-track positions, have increasingly diminished expectations of knowing the security that comes with being a part of the permanent faculty. Their best hope is to land a sabbatical replacement position or some other type of limited-term or contract appointment that might eventually lead to a more secure long-term position; however, for most of these academic job-seekers their lives as low-paid, overworked itinerant sessional instructors (often travelling from one location to another to teach a single course) are structurally doomed to continue.

As for the students – another group clearly being harmed – the price they pay for the mess that is today's higher education is often debilitating. In Canada, at Ontario universities, to take just one province, over the past thirty to thirty-five years tuition has doubled while government support for higher education has been cut in half. At Lakehead this has meant a drop from somewhere over 80 per cent of the total university budget to government's contribution of around 42 or 43 per cent. I personally know several graduate students enrolled in doctoral programs in three Southern Ontario universities whose final postgraduate bill of indebtedness will be in the area of $50,000, with at least one student's final sum totalling somewhere north of $70,000. These figures accumulated despite the students' employment in a series of part-time undergraduate jobs or full-time summer work, as well as continuing postings as teaching/research assistants and several sessional instructorships. Students are going into serious debt to pay for having fun in the edutainment party atmosphere. Party On! may have quite a different meaning for these students, whose education has cost them so dearly at such a young age.

The Way Forward

To ensure student well-being and to protect and nurture scholarship, universities must make drastic changes. Cleaning up the mess will not be easy. The way forward includes establishing a higher learning context of sociability that connects the university to the many diverse communities that surround it. This involves changing routines and habits. Colleges and universities could and should lead the way in fossil-fuel divestment, a fiscal decision that would offer leadership in helping us change wasteful and environmentally disastrous lifestyles. Becoming more aware of the many ways in which we humans have created debilitating environmental impacts is both essential and inevitable.

The dependency on fossil fuels is only one problem. Another is the use and waste of water – an issue that is beginning to enter our consciousness with reduced supplies and shortages both globally and here in North America. In June 2016 a U.S. plan to draw water from the Great Lakes–St. Lawrence River basin, a departure from an agreement banning such diversions, raised concerns among many Canadians.[10] Water shortages and droughts brought on by human interference with nature over the years (dams, floodgates, irrigation schemes, and many other water diversions) have become commonplace in the United States, especially in California and other Western states. Again, the university, with its many research scientists and their diverse scholarly and academic training, has the potential to play a leading role as a caretaker of our water. Water shortages, fossil-fuel dependence, and many other climate-change challenges might well be better addressed by a reorganized university structure, possibly along the lines of the Plymouth State experiment. With regard to conserving our natural resources, we all want and need policies and programs that promise and deliver an equal share.

Another problem in the system is the deeply embedded inequality. One wonders how many more learned books and articles we are going to need before we begin to connect higher education with growing inequality in a way that sparks remedial action. Ed Miliband's "The Inequality Problem,"[11] for instance, puts the lie to the argument that increased inequality is a corollary of economic success. It is time that we began to take steps to do something about this fundamental problem that intersects with and runs across social class, gender, and ethnic/racial lines. It is an inequality that is bedrock to and reproduces the capitalist system founded upon it. Certainly by now it should be clear that further technological developments and refinements will provide neither short- nor long-term answers.

The notion that somehow high-tech education will provide an easy fix for the many inequities that make up this fundamental inequality is both facile and wrongheaded. Kentaro Toyama's article "Why Technology Alone Won't Fix Schools" addresses this issue. For more than a decade Toyama has "designed, studied, and taught educational technology in different parts of the world" – in Bangalore, India, in rural Uganda, and in Seattle, Washington. What he found with respect to all the projects in these three locations, what they all had in common, is adherence to "the law of amplification: Technology's primary effect is to amplify human forces, so in education, technologies amplify whatever pedagogical capacity is already there."[12] Take his Seattle site, for example, the school where he worked, Lakeside (where Bill Gates is a recognizable graduate). It has a student population that comes from the professional families of Amazon and Microsoft executives. The very latest technology is omnipresent for these students both at home and at the expensive school they attend. As a tutor for these students of privilege, Toyama found many differences among them in their academic struggles – some were overmatched in their honours classes, some were overextended in extracurricular activities, some were homework procrastinators who needed prodding, and others were simply just lazy or disinterested. But despite their several differences they had one extremely important thing in common: parents willing (and able) to pay for "extra adult supervision" because they wanted "more adult guidance" for their kids. They and other parents at other sites in both developed and developing economies were valuing quality time with adults over technology. The parents had come to the realization that more computers and more high-tech education with the machine as centrepiece are not the answer – technology will not solve our inequality problems in school or in the world outside academia.

Toyama's conclusion emphasizes the folly of encouraging a technological fix for education: "If educational inequality is the main issue, then no amount of digital technology will turn things around. . . . Technology amplifies preexisting differences in wealth and achievement. . . . Inequity in educational opportunity isn't a problem that technology can fix. Without addressing the underlying socio-economic chasm, technology by itself doesn't bridge the gap, it only jacks it further apart."[13]

In the end, people involved in college and university teaching need to create a higher education version of thinking and acting locally at the classroom level – a vision that will move us towards the goal of connecting both global and local awareness and action for change. A first step in beginning to fix our universities is to renew and increase our reliance on fired-up teachers (not necessarily Ph.D.-certified) interacting with students face-to-face in classroom settings. Whether this takes place in large lecture halls with plenty of smaller group tutorials to serve large enrolments, or in seminar rooms with a relatively small number of students, matters little. We need to focus on recovering scholarly conversation unmediated by high-tech machinery. To do this we must, as professors, give up a good deal of the control we continue to exercise. We must redouble our efforts to talk to our students about what we know and the research we are engaged with in a manner that brings them into the conversation as fully participating seekers of knowledge.

If we take up this challenge, both parties, students and professors, can leave behind our concerned anxiousness about grades and certification, as well as edutainment preoccupation, and begin to build intellectually invigorating communities of interest that connect learners in their localities with the wider world beyond.

Notes

ONE: The University from the Inside-Out

1 Sherry Turkle, *Alone Together: Why We Expect More from Technology and Less from Each Other* (New York: Basic Books, 2011); and Turkle, *Reclaiming Conversation: The Power of Talk in a Digital Age* (New York: Penguin, 2015).

2 Naomi Klein, *This Changes Everything: Capitalism vs. the Climate* (Toronto: Knopf Canada, 2014).

3 See Tony E. Adams, Stacy Holman Jones, and Carolyn Ellis, *Autoethnography: Understanding Qualitative Research* (Oxford: Oxford University Press, 2014), for a comprehensive bibliography on this research approach.

4 C. Wright Mills, *The Sociological Imagination* (London: Oxford University Press, 1959), p.6.

5 Ibid., p.55.

6 Will Ferguson, *419* (New York: Viking Books/Random House, 2012).

7 Noam Chomsky, *American Power and the New Mandarins* (New York: Random House, 1969), p.343.

8 Thomas S. Kuhn, *The Structure of Scientific Revolutions* (Chicago: University of Chicago Press, 1962).

9 Hayden White, *Metahistory: The Historical Imagination in Nineteenth-Century Europe* (Baltimore: Johns Hopkins University Press, 1975).

10 Ida M. Tarbell, *The History of the Standard Oil Company* (New York: Cosimo Classics Publishers, 2010 [1904]); Upton Sinclair, *The Goose-Step: A Study of American Education* (Pasadena, Cal.: n.p., 1923).

11 See Robert E.L. Faris, *Chicago Sociology 1920–1932* (Chicago: University of Chicago Press, 1970); Martin Bulmer, *The Chicago School of Sociology: Institutionalization, Diversity, and the Rise of Sociological Research*, 2nd ed. (Chicago: University of Chicago Press, 1986); Andrew Abbott, *Department and Discipline: Chicago Sociology at One Hundred* (Chicago: University of Chicago Press, 1999).

12 See, for example, Dorothy E. Smith, *The Everyday World as Problematic: A Feminist Sociology* (Lebanon, N.H.: Northeastern University Press [University Press of New England], 1987); and Smith, *The Conceptual Practices of Power: A Feminist Sociology of Knowledge* (Toronto: University of Toronto Press, 1990).

13 Mills, *Sociological Imagination*, p.8.

14 Ibid., p.6.

TWO: Campus Parking and the Car as a Third Place

1 Clark Kerr, *The Uses of the University* (New York: Harper and Row, 1964), p.20.
2 In two previous books I developed some of the perspectives and arguments used in this chapter: Randle W. Nelsen, *Fun & Games & Higher Education: The Lonely Crowd Revisited* (Toronto: Between the Lines, 2007); and Nelsen, *Life of the Party: A Study in Sociability, Community, and Social Inequality* (Toronto: Between the Lines, 2012). In places here I use the same or similar wording found in those two books.
3 Information provided here with respect to parking regulations, fees, among other things, as well as more general information regarding school demographics, can be found online at the respective websites of each university.
4 Expansion in the amount of land devoted to providing parking on university campuses is symptomatic of what is happening outside the walls of the university. At the end of 2015, CBC News was reporting that 30 per cent of land space in Toronto was being used for parking.
5 Ray Oldenburg, *The Great Good Place: Cafés, Coffee Shops, Bookstores, Bars, Hair Salons, and Other Hangouts at the Heart of a Community* (New York: Marlowe & Company, 1997), p.217.
6 See Nelsen, *Fun & Games & Higher Education*, ch. 3.
7 Daniel I. Vieyra, "The Architecture of America's Roadside Lodging from Its Beginning to the Interstate Era," unpublished Ph.D. dissertation, Case Western Reserve University, Cleveland, 1995, p.21.
8 Arthur R.M. Lower, *Canadians in the Making: A Social History of Canada* (Toronto: Longmans, Green and Company, 1958), p.425.
9 Oldenberg, *Great Good Place*, pp.290–91.
10 Ibid., p.216.
11 Reuel Denney, *The Astonished Muse* (Chicago: University of Chicago Press,1964 [1957]), p.142.
12 Ibid., p.145.
13 See Nelsen, *Life of the Party*; Nelsen, *Fun & Games & Higher Education*. In a detailed analysis of the football tailgate party in *Fun & Games* I demonstrate how automobility and social mobility come together.
14 Edward T. Hall, *The Hidden Dimension* (New York: Anchor, 1990 [1966]), p.145.
15 Oldenburg, *Great Good Place*, p.152.
16 See Robert D. Putnam, *Bowling Alone: The Collapse and Revival of American Community* (New York: Simon & Schuster, 2000).
17 Oldenburg, *Great Good Place*, p.13.
18 David Gelles, Hiroko Tabuchi, and Matthew Dolan, "The Weak Spot under the Hood," *The New York Times*, Sept. 27, 2015, p.1.
19 Ibid., p.4. I shall forego further discussion of important safety and security issues, as well as further speculation as to the potential role to be played by individual amateurs in monitoring and protecting us from the large-scale organized greed of profit-making professionals.
20 Oldenburg, *Great Good Place*, pp.43, 44, and see the rest of his chapter 3 for more detail.
21 See Nelsen, *Fun & Games & Higher Education*, ch. 5; and *Life of the Party*, for not only football tailgates but also other kinds of parties.
22 See Nelsen, *Life of the Party*, ch. 2 (pp.19–32), especially p.23.
23 Nelsen, *Fun & Games & Higher Education*, p.79.
24 Ibid., p.82.

THREE: Parents and Pedagogy

1 Christopher Lasch, *The Culture of Narcissism: American Life in an Age of Diminishing Expectations* (New York: W.W. Norton & Company, 1979), pp.154–55.

2 Ibid., p.156.

3 Ibid., pp.161–62.

4 Benjamin Spock, *The Common Sense Book of Baby and Child Care* (New York: Duell, Sloan and Pearce, 1946). The tremendous popularity of this book led to several updated editions.

5 Lasch, *Culture of Narcissism*, p.163.

6 Ibid., pp.166–67.

7 Edgar Z. Friedenberg, *Coming of Age in America: Growth and Acquiescence* (New York: Random House, 1963), p.76.

8 Neil Postman, *The Disappearance of Childhood* (New York: Delacorte, 1982). In selected portions of my remarks here on childhood with regard to technological change, parenting, and the school I use similar, and at times the same, wording as appeared in Randle W. Nelsen, "The End of Childhood: Technological Change, Parenting and the School," *Canadian Review of Sociology and Anthropology* 22, 2 (1985): 303–10, which was reprinted as ch. 5 in Randle W. Nelsen, *Miseducating: Death of the Sensible* (Kingston, Ont.: Cedarcreek Publications, 1991).

9 See David Elkind, *The Hurried Child: Growing Up Too Fast Too Soon* (Boston: Da Capo Press, 1981).

10 Ashley Stahl, "Five Reasons Why Helicopter Parents Are Sabotaging Their Children's Careers," *The Huffington Post*, Aug. 14, 2015.

11 Ibid.

12 Hara Estroff Marano, "Helicopter Parenting – It's Worse Than You Think," *Psychology Today*, Jan. 31, 2014, www.psychologytoday.com.

13 Alfie Kohn, "Debunking the Myth of the 'Helicopter Parent': The Pernicious Cultural Biases behind a Collegiate Urban Legend," *Salon*, Sept. 4, 2015.

14 Ibid.

15 See Pierre Bourdieu, "Cultural Reproduction and Social Reproduction," in *Power and Ideology in Education,* ed. Jerome Karabel and A.H. Halsey (New York: Oxford University Press, 1977).

16 Kohn, "Debunking the Myth of the 'Helicopter parent.'"

17 See Conor Friedersdorf, "Working Mom Arrested for Letting Her 9-Year-Old Play Alone at Park," *The Atlantic*, July 15, 2014, www.theatlantic.com.

18 Holly Blackford, "Playground Panopticism: Ring-Around-the-Children, a Pocketful of Women," *Childhood* 11:2 (May 2004): 227–49. See also Heather G. Kaplan, "Visualizing Spaces of Childhood," Occasional Paper Series, no. 31, New York: Bank Street College of Education, n.d.; and Michel Foucault, *Discipline and Punish: The Birth of the Prison* (New York: Viking Press, 1995 [1975]).

19 Postman, *Disappearance of Childhood*, ch. 6.

20 Valerie Suransky Polakow, *The Erosion of Childhood* (Chicago: University of Chicago Press, 1982), p.179. Polakow's book was originally published under the name Suransky Polakow.

21 Marie Winn, *Children without Childhood* (New York: Pantheon, 1983), p.133.

22 See Marshall McLuhan, *Understanding Media: The Extensions of Man* (Toronto: McGraw-Hill, 1964); and Harold Innis, *Empire and Communications* (Toronto: University of Toronto Press, 1950).

23 Marie Winn, *The Plug-in Drug* (New York: Viking, 1978), p.6.

24 Dave McGinn, "Parents, It's Not Just the Kids Who Need to Step away from the Screens," *The Globe and Mail*, Aug. 28, 2015, p.L3.

25 Greg Lukianoff and Jonathan Haidt, "The Coddling of the American Mind," *The Atlantic*, September 2015, p.44.

26 Ibid.

27 Ibid., pp.45, 47–48.

28 Ibid., pp.50, 49.

29 Mark Leviton, "The Kids Are All Right: David Lancy Questions Our Assumptions about Parenting," *The Sun Magazine*, 482 (February 2016), p.6, thesunmagazine.org. I draw upon a feature interview with *The Sun Magazine*'s Leviton to present some of these opinions as they relate to this chapter.

30 Ibid., p.6.

31 See Jeff Schmidt, *Disciplined Minds: A Critical Look at Salaried Professionals and the Soul-Battering System That Shapes Their Lives* (New York: Rowman & Littlefield, 2000).

32 Leviton, "The Kids Are All Right," p.10.

33 Ibid., p.10.

34 Ibid., p.11.

35 Laurie Monsebraaten, "Internet Takes a Big Bite Out of Food Budget," *Toronto Star*, Feb. 2, 2016, p.GT1.

36 Louise Brown, "Push for Aboriginal Higher Education," *Toronto Star*, Feb. 2, 2016, pp.GT1, GT3.

FOUR: Professionals and Professionalism

1 Josh Logue, "Losing His Job for Teaching Too Well," *Inside Higher Ed*, Oct. 13, 2015, www.insidehighered.com. The quotations in the following three paragraphs are from this same source.

2 See Randle W. Nelsen, "The Military-Industrial-University Complex and Social Science: A Brief History and Current Update of a Professional Contribution to War," in *Educating for Peace in a Time of "Permanent War": Are Schools Part of the Solution or the Problem?* ed. P.R. Carr and B.J. Porfilio (London: Routledge, 2012), p.152.

3 Martin Nicolaus, "The Professional Organization of Sociology: A View from Below," *The Antioch Review* 29 (Fall 1969), pp.382–83.

4 The past forty-five years have seen changes to these arrangements, but the hierarchical and bureaucratic structure of the professional association remains.

5 See Alan Wolfe, "Practicing the Pluralism We Preach: Internal Processes in the American Political Science Association," *The Antioch Review* 29 (Fall 1969): 353–73; Daniel Bell, *The End of Ideology: On the Exhaustion of Political Ideas in the Fifties* (Glencoe, Ill.: Free Press, 1960), p.73, for the full context of this statement.

6 Wolfe, "Practicing the Pluralism We Preach," p.370.

7 See, for example, Dusky Lee Smith, "Sociology and the Rise of Corporate Capitalism," *Science and Society* 29 (Fall 1965): 401–18; Herman Schwendinger and Julia R. Schwendinger, *The Sociologists of the Chair: A Radical Analysis of the Formative Years of North American Sociology 1883–1922* (New York: Basic Books, 1974); Randle W. Nelsen, "Growth of the Modern University and the Development of a Sociology of Higher Education in the United States," unpublished Ph.D. dissertation, McMaster University, Hamilton, Ont., 1975; and more recently, Andrew Abbott, *Department and Discipline: Chicago Sociology at One Hundred* (Chicago: University of Chicago Press, 1999).

8 See the American Sociological Association (ASA) website.

9 Ibid., ASA Rose Series. Emphases added.

10 Ibid. Emphases added.

11 Diana Crane, "The Gatekeepers of Science: Some Factors Affecting the Selection of Articles for Scientific Journals," *The American Sociologist* 2 (November 1967): 195–201.

12 See Russell Sage Foundation (RSF) website, "About the Foundation."

13 Jay Schulman, Carol Brown, and Roger Kahn, "Report on the Russell Sage Foundation," *The Insurgent Sociologist* 2, 4 (1972), p.2.

14 Nelsen, "Growth of the Modern University," p.213.

15 Schulman, Brown, and Kahn, "Report on the Russell Sage Foundation," p.22.

16 Ibid., p.27.

17 Ibid., see pp.30, 31–32.

18 Ibid., see pp.3, 33.

19 See Christopher Jencks and David Riesman, *The Academic Revolution* (Garden City, N.J.: Doubleday, 1968). Later Thomas J. Scheff would lead other analysts in describing affinities and groupings within these racecourses as "academic gangs."

20 See Jencks and Riesman, *Academic Revolution*; Christopher Jencks et al., *Inequality: A Reassessment of the Effect of Family and Schooling in America* (New York: Basic Books, 1972); Nelsen, "Growth of the Modern University," pp.202–4.

21 Antony J. Puddephatt and Neil McLaughlin, "Critical Nexus or Pluralist Discipline? Institutional Ambivalence and the Future of Canadian Sociology," *Canadian Review of Sociology* 52, 3 (2015), p.312.

22 Ibid., p.317.

23 Ibid., pp.317, 322, 323.

24 Ibid., p.323. Emphasis added.

25 Ibid., pp.328–29.

26 See Burton R. Clark, *Educating the Expert Society* (San Francisco: Chandler, 1962), p.288; Nelsen, "Growth of the Modern University," as written with only minor wording changes on pp.204–5.

27 I have made this argument in other places using similar wording and these same examples regarding reference group switching as it pertains to blocking fundamental social change. See Randle W. Nelsen, "The Community College Con: 'Changing Your Life through Learning,'" in *Work, Occupations and Professionalization,* ed. S.A. Bosanac and M.A. Jacobs (Whitby, Ont.: de Sitter, 2010), ch. 11; Nelsen, "Military-Industrial-University Complex," p.155; Nelsen, "Growth of the Modern University," pp.207–9.

28 Alvin W. Gouldner, "Anti-Minotaur: The Myth of a Value-Free Sociology," *Social Problems* 9 (Winter 1962), p.206.

29 Jencks and Riesman, *Academic Revolution*, is especially good at shifting responsibility in a way that emphasizes the failings of particular individuals; Clark, *Educating the Expert Society*, is adept at making vague and ill-defined references to "society" as the locus of social problems. This sentence as well as much of the wording in the previous paragraph and the last four paragraphs of this chapter originally appeared in Nelsen, "Growth of the Modern University," pp.221–23.

30 See Noam Chomsky, *American Power and the New Mandarins* (New York: Random House, 1969), p.345.

31 See Sidney M. Willhelm, "Scientific Unaccountability and Moral Accountability," in *The New Sociology: Essays in Social Science and Social Theory,* ed. Irving Louis Horowitz (New York: Oxford University Press, 1964), p.184.

32 For more on this reading of Weber's sociology and his views, see J.P. Mayer, *Max Weber and German Politics* (London: Faber and Faber, 1955), pp.88, 76.

33 Chomsky, *American Power and the New Mandarins*, p.345. The following (p.324) indicates what Chomsky has in mind when he refers to "the responsibility of intellectuals": "Intellectuals are in a position to expose the lies of governments, to analyze actions according to their causes and motives and often hidden intentions. In the Western world, at least, they have the power that comes from political liberty, from access to information and freedom of expression. . . . The responsibilities of intellectuals, then, are much deeper than . . . the 'responsibility of peoples', given the unique privileges that intellectuals enjoy."

34 See Michael Burawoy, "For Public Sociology," ASA Presidential Address, *American Sociological Review* 70 (February 2005): 4–28; Ben Agger, *Public Sociology: From Social Facts to Literary Acts* (Lanham, Md.: Roman and Littlefield, 2007).

35 Nicolaus, "Professional Organization of Sociology," p.387.

FIVE: Edubusiness and Edutainment

1 See Michael Locke, "The Decline of Universities with the Rise of Edubis," in *Inside Canadian Universities: Another Day at the Plant*, ed. Randle W. Nelsen (Kingston, Ont.: Cedarcreek Publications, 1997), p.13. This article was reprinted from *Society/ Société* 14, 2 (1990) and used with the permission of the journal. It was first published in Western News, University of Western Ontario, Jan. 19, 1989, when Locke was a professor and Killam Fellow in the Department of Zoology, Faculty of Science.

2 Locke, "Decline of Universities with the Rise of Edubis," pp.13–14.

3 Ibid., p.16.

4 Ibid., p.17.

5 Ibid., p.19.

6 See Norene Pupo, "The Postwar University in Canada and the Need for Skilled Labour: The Waterloo Example," in *Reading, Writing and Riches: Education and the Socio-Economic Order in North America*, ed. Randle W. Nelsen and David A. Nock (Kitchener, Ont.: Between the Lines, 1978), pp.138–70. This article was based on her doctoral dissertation at McMaster University, Hamilton, Ont.

7 Pupo, quoted in Randle W. Nelsen, *Schooling as Entertainment: Corporate Education Meets Popular Culture* (Kingston, Ont.: Cedarcreek Publications, 2002), p.126.

8 Ibid.

9 Ibid., pp.126–127; see also Pupo, "Postwar University in Canada and the Need for Skilled Labour," pp.138–139.

10 Pupo, "Postwar University in Canada and the Need for Skilled Labour," as quoted in *Reading, Writing, and Riches*, ed. Nelsen and Nock, p.163.

11 I draw upon and repeat some of my past writing on early university-business connections to offer a complementary perspective that summarizes the U.S. case.

12 See Merle Curti and Roderick Nash, *Philanthropy in the Shaping of American Higher Education* (New Brunswick, N.J.: Rutgers University Press, 1965), p.43.

13 Ibid., p.745.

14 Neil W. Hamilton, *Zealotry and Academic Freedom: A Legal and Historical Perspective* (Piscataway, N.J.: Transaction Publishers, 1995), p.13.

15 See "Ward Churchill," entry in *Wikipedia*, for references and more detail.

16 See Donald Wright, *The Professionalization of History in English Canada* (Toronto: University of Toronto Press, 2005).

17 See Michiel Horn, *Academic Freedom in Canada: A History* (Toronto: University of Toronto Press, 1999).

18 Randle W. Nelsen, "The Military-Industrial-University Complex and Social Science: A Brief History and Current Update of a Professional Contribution to War," in *Educating for Peace in a Time of "Permanent War": Are Schools Part of the Solution or the Problem?* ed. P.R. Carr and B.J. Porfilio (London: Routledge, 2012), p.156.

19 Ibid., p.157.

20 See "University Inc. Compromises Academic Freedom," *CAUT Bulletin*, November 2015, p.A7.

21 See "University of Calgary under Fire over Ties with Energy Company," *CAUT Bulletin*, November 2015, p.A7.

22 For quotes in this paragraph, see Robin Vose, "The Problem with Corporate Influence on Canadian Campuses," *CAUT/ACPPU Bulletin* 62, 9 (November 2015), p.A3.

23 See Jane Mayer, *Dark Money: The Hidden History of the Billionaires behind the Rise of the Radical Right* (New York: Knopf Doubleday, 2016); Connor Gibson, "To Charles Koch, Universities Are Propaganda Machines," *The Huffington Post: The Blog*, Jan. 27, 2016; and Gibson, "To Charles Koch, Professors Are Lobbyists," *The Huffington Post: The Blog*, Jan. 28, 2016. Mayer is an award-winning investigative journalist and longtime staff writer for *The New Yorker*. Gibson is a Greenpeace researcher with the organization's Investigations team.

24 See Gibson, "To Charles Koch, Universities Are Propaganda Machines." The quote within the quote is from David Packard, former Deputy Secretary of Defense.

25 Gibson, "To Charles Koch, Universities Are Propaganda Machines." Foundation philanthropy to academia is not new. See, for example, early donations of the Carnegie Foundation, stretching back to its establishment in 1902.

26 Mayer, *Dark Money*, p.150.

27 See Gibson, "To Charles Koch, Professors Are Lobbyists."

28 Mayer, *Dark Money*, p.56.

29 See Gibson, "To Charles Koch, Professors Are Lobbyists," from Mayer, *Dark Money*, pp.103–4.

30 See Gibson, "To Charles Koch, Professors Are Lobbyists."

31 Mayer, *Dark Money*, p.108.

32 See Gibson, "To Charles Koch, Professors Are Lobbyists"; and Mayer, *Dark Money*, p.365. On Sobel textbooks, see James D. Gwartney, Richard L. Stroup, Russell S. Sobel, and David A. Macpherson, eds., *Economics: Private and Public Choice* (Boston: Cengage Learning, 2010). See also S. Russell Sobel, ed., *Unleashing Capitalism: Why Prosperity Stops at the West Virginia Border and How to Fix It* (Wheeling: Public Policy Foundation of West Virginia, 2007); and Sobel, *The Rule of Law: Perspectives on Legal and Judicial Reform in West Virginia* (Wheeling: Public Policy Foundation of West Virginia, 2009).

33 Gibson, "To Charles Koch, Professors Are Lobbyists," drawing upon Mayer, *Dark Money*, pp.155, 171. The story of Charles Koch and his university philanthropy continues, especially with regard to the work that his money is backing at George Mason University. Some of the most recent material is to be found in a news article and discussion by Colleen Flaherty, "Seeking a Pause on Scalia Law," *Inside Higher Ed*, May 5, 2016, www.insidehighered.com. The Flaherty article focuses on the strings attached to Koch's gifting and the impact of these strings on university governance. The article stresses how the "George Mason Faculty Senate, citing provisions that professors say give inappropriate influence to donors, asks institution to hold off in renaming law school after the late Antonin Scalia under Charles Koch-funded agreement." Using the university as a political football in Koch's case means that he is dragging the university along in support of his far-right, conservative political agenda. There is potential harm in further politicizing the academy, shaping it to fit the political orientation and views of donors.

34 See Eugene F. Provenzo, Jr., *Video Kids: Making Sense of Nintendo* (Cambridge, Mass.: Harvard University Press, 1991).

35 See Peter McLaren, *Life in Schools: An Introduction to Critical Pedagogy in the Foundations of Education* (Toronto: Irwin, 1989).

36 See Michael Moore, *Cheating 101: The Benefits and Fundamentals of Earning the Easy "A"* (n.p.: Moore Publishing, 1991), and commented upon in *Harper's Magazine*, April 1992, p.20.

37 For biographical and donation information, see "Phil Knight," entry in *Wikipedia*. For updates on donations to cancer research see Laura Lorenzetti, "Nike's Phil Knight Donating $500 Million to Cancer Research," *Fortune.com*, June 25, 2015.

38 Lorenzetti, "Nike's Phil Knight"; and "Phil Knight," *Wikipedia*, with reference to both the football facility and the basketball arena.

39 For information on the Mariota Center, see "Nike Co-founder, Phil Knight, Funds University of Oregon's Advanced New Sports Science Complex," *SportTechie Newletter*, 2015, www.sporttechie.com.

40 Josh Peter, "Behind Oregon's (Phil) Knight in Shining Armor," *USA Today*, Dec. 30, 2014, www.usatoday.com.

41 I have not provided detail on these matters here, but there has been no shortage of criticism of Knight and Nike's business practices, in particular dealing with the com-

pany's offshore factories. Telling criticism can be found in: Naomi Klein, *No Logo: Taking Aim at the Brand Bullies* (Toronto: Viking Canada, 2009 [1999]); J.B. Strasser and Laurie Becklund, *Swoosh: The Unauthorized Story of Nike and the Men Who Played There* (New York: HarperBusiness, 1993); and Michael Moore, *Downsize This! Random Threats from an Unarmed American* (New York: Harper, 1997) (in which the author refers to Knight as a "corporate crook").

42 See Michael Oriard, *Reading Football: How the Popular Press Created an American Spectacle* (Chapel Hill: University of North Carolina Press, 1993), pp.61–62, 101; Randle W. Nelsen, *Fun & Games & Higher Education: The Lonely Crowd Revisited* (Toronto: Between the Lines, 2007), pp.67–68.

43 Michael Russell, "University of Oregon Ranked among Nation's Top Party Schools," 2014, http://connect.oregonlive.com/staff/mrussell/posts.html.

44 This assessment is based on a 2010 survey of marketing practices of fifty-four English-speaking sociology departments in Canada conducted with my colleague Antony Puddephatt.

45 Antony J. Puddephatt and Randle W. Nelsen, "The Promise of a Sociology Degree in Canadian Higher Education," *Canadian Review of Sociology* 47, 4 (2010), p.422.

46 See Andy Thomason, "This Is How Students Cheat in MOOCs," *The Chronicle of Higher Education*, Aug. 25, 2015, reporting on research by Curtis G. Northcutt, Andrew D. Ho, and Isaac L. Chuang, "Detecting and Preventing 'Multiple Account' Cheating in Massive Open Online Courses," working paper, published online, Aug. 24, 2015.

47 Kyle Carsten Wyatt, "Busted," *The Walrus* (November 2015), p.36.

48 Ibid., p.38.

49 Ibid., p.39. As yet, there is no reliable data on professorial plagiarism.

50 Ibid., p.38.

51 James J. Farrell, *The Nature of College: College Culture, Consumer Culture and the Environment* (Minneapolis, Minn.: Milkweed Editions, 2010), p.1.

52 Ibid., pp.4–7.

53 See Elizabeth A. Armstrong and Laura T. Hamilton, *Paying for the Party: How College Maintains Inequality* (Cambridge, Mass. and London: Harvard University Press, 2013), p.2.

54 Ibid., p.84.

55 Ibid., pp.11–12.

56 See Matthew Reisz, "Social Arts Trample Liberal Arts," *Times Higher Education*, 2013, www.timeshighereducation.com, quoting from Armstrong and Hamilton, *Paying for the Party*.

57 See Reisz, "Social Arts Trample Liberal Arts."

58 Ibid., with quotes from Armstrong and Hamilton, *Paying for the Party*.

SIX: Educators and Education at a Distance

1 Randle W. Nelsen, "Reading, Writing and Relationships among the Electronic Zealots: Distance Education and the Traditional University," in *Inside Canadian Universities: Another Day at the Plant*, ed. Randle W. Nelsen (Kingston, Ont.: Cedarcreek Publications, 1997), p.187.

2 John Ralston Saul, *The Unconscious Civilization* (Concord, Ont.: Anansi, 1995), p.15.

3 Laura Penny, *More Money Than Brains: Why School Sucks, College Is Crap, & Idiots Think They're Right* (Toronto: McClelland & Stewart, 2010), p.192.

4 See Lakehead University calendars, 1995–96, 2015–16.

5 See Lakehead University calendar, 1995–96, p.239.

6 Nelsen, "Reading, Writing and Relationships among the Electronic Zealots," pp.196–97.

7 Ibid., pp.191–93. In this and the following three paragraphs, to illustrate the changeover from in-person courses to education at a distance I am using statistics

from my own sociology department. Note that I am using nearly identical wording from my mid-1990s research and writing,

8 Bruce Powe, "Wired to Distraction," *University Affairs*, December 1995, p.11.

9 J.W. Murphy, "The Sociology of Knowledge and the Use of Computers in the Classroom," Toronto: unpublished paper, n.d., p.5.

10 Powe, "Wired to Distraction," p.10.

11 Theodore Roszak, *The Cult of Information: The Folklore of Computers and the True Art of Thinking* (New York: Pantheon, 1986), p.88.

12 Neil Postman, *Morningside*, interview with Peter Gzowski, CBC-Radio, Dec. 15, 1992. This paragraph, with minor changes, as well as much of the next paragraph can be found in Nelsen, "Reading, Writing and Relationships among the Electronic Zealots," pp.200, 202.

13 Neil Postman, *Technopoly: The Surrender of Culture to Technology* (New York: Random House, 1993), pp.71, 107.

14 Sherry Turkle, *Alone Together: Why We Expect More from Technology and Less from Each Other* (New York: Basic Books, 2011), p.x.

15 Ibid.

16 Ibid., p.xi.

17 Ibid., p.xii.

18 Ibid. Emphasis added.

19 See David Riesman, Reuel Denney, and Nathan Glazer, *The Lonely Crowd: A Study of the Changing American Character* (New Haven, Conn.: Yale University Press, 1950).

20 See Hal Niedzviecki, *Hello, I'm Special: How Individuality Became the New Conformity* (Toronto: Penguin, 2004).

21 See the submission by Carl Straumsheim, "Partial Credit: The 2015 Survey of Faculty Attitudes on Technology," *Inside Higher Ed*, Oct. 14, 2015, for survey data and his review.

22 Clifford Stoll, *Silicon Snake Oil: Second Thoughts on the Information Highway* (New York: Doubleday, 1995), p.118.

23 Turkle, *Alone Together*, pp.11, 289, 295.

24 Carlos Spoerhase, "Seminar Versus MOOC," *New Left Review* 96 (November-December 2015), p.77, quoting Bromwich, "The Hi-Tech Mess of Higher Education," *New York Review of Books*, Aug. 14, 2014.

25 Spoerhase, "Seminar Versus MOOC," pp.78, 79.

26 Ibid., p.79.

27 Ibid., p.80.

28 Ibid., p.81.

29 Ibid., pp.81–82.

SEVEN: Classroom Practice and Student-Friendly Suggestions

1 William Deresiewicz, "The Neoliberal Arts: How College Sold Its Soul to the Market," *Harper's*, September 2015, p.26.

2 Ibid., p.27.

3 See Paulo Freire, *Pedagogy of the Oppressed*, trans. Myra Bergman Ramos (New York: Herder and Herder, 1971); also bell hooks, *Teaching to Transgress: Education as the Practice of Freedom* (New York: Routledge, 1994).

4 See Deresiewicz, "Neoliberal Arts," p.31.

5 James J. Farrell, *The Nature of College: College Culture, Consumer Culture and the Environment* (Minneapolis, Minn.: Milkweed Editions, 2010), p.10.

6 Ibid., p.13.

7 See Edward Gross, "Universities as Organizations: A Research Approach," *American Sociological Review* 33 (1968): 518–44, for an early example of this documentation.

8 See, for example, Stuart Smith, *Report: Commission of Inquiry on Canadian University Education* (Ottawa: Association of Universities and Colleges in Canada, 1991).

9 See Nikhil Goyal, *One Size Does Not Fit All: A Student's Assessment of School* (Roslyn Heights, N.Y.: Alternative Education Resource Organization, 2012).

10 David F. Noble, *Digital Diploma Mills: The Automation of Higher Education* (Toronto: Between the Lines, 2002), p.2.

11 I have reproduced this list, with minor changes in wording, from previous writing. See Rebecca Collins-Nelsen and Randle W. Nelsen, "Developing a User-Friendly, Community-Based Higher Education," in *Social Context Reform: A Pedagogy of Equity and Opportunity*, ed. P.L. Thomas, Brad Porfilio, Julie Gorlewski, and Paul R. Carr (New York and London: Routledge, 2014), p.195.

12 For greater detail regarding this less-structured classroom "experiment," see Randle W. Nelsen, "Reading, Writing and Relationship: Towards Overcoming the Hidden Curriculum of Gender, Ethnicity, and Socio-Economic Class," *Interchange* 12, 2–3 (1981), pp.229–42. In some places here I have used the same, or in some cases very similar, wording as in the original. Some of this original material, in less detailed form, can also be found in Collins-Nelsen and Nelsen, "Developing a User-Friendly, Community-Based Higher Education."

13 Nelsen, "Reading, Writing, and Relationship," p.182. The quotes are taken from an in-class recording made with the approval of all class members, Sept. 12, 1979.

14 See Noble, *Digital Diploma Mills*; Abraham H. Maslow, *Motivation and Personality*, 2nd ed. (New York: Harper & Row,1970).

15 Nelsen, "Reading, Writing, and Relationship," p.237.

16 For writeups of these two cases, see Nelsen, "Reading, Writing, and Relationship," pp.200–1; Collins-Nelsen and Nelsen, "Developing a User-Friendly, Community-Based Higher Education," p.191.

17 See Debbie Storrs, "Teaching Mills in Tokyo: Developing a Sociological Imagination through Storytelling," *Teaching Sociology* 37, 1 (2009): 31–46. Storrs insightfully conveys the pedagogy of storytelling in her account of how she taught the sociology of Mills to students in Tokyo.

18 The story outlined in this and the following paragraph, along with comments regarding its pedagogical relevance, also appears (with some alterations in wording) in Collins-Nelsen and Nelsen, "Developing a User-Friendly, Community-Based Higher Education," pp.193–94.

19 Clay Shirky, *Here Comes Everybody: The Power of Organizing without Organizations* (New York: Penguin, 2008).

20 Ibid., pp.25–80.

21 Jo-Ann Archibald, "Q'um Q'um Xiiem," *Indigenous Storywork: Educating the Heart, Mind, Body, and Spirit* (Vancouver: UBC Press, 2008), p.ix.

22 Ibid.

23 Ibid., p.x.

24 Ibid., p.115.

25 Ibid., p.131.

26 Ibid., p.133.

27 Ibid., p.139.

28 Matthew B. Crawford, *Shop Class as Soulcraft: An Inquiry into the Value of Work* (New York: Penguin, 2010), p.57.

29 Ibid., p.56.

30 Naomi Klein, *This Changes Everything: Capitalism vs. the Climate* (Toronto: Knopf Canada, 2014). Much of what follows I have put together as a result of reading this important book.

31 See *The Leap Manifesto: A Call for a Canada Based on Caring for the Earth and One Another*, leapmanifesto.org, 2015. I urge all readers of this book to consult the manifesto as a way of learning about the environmental challenges we face and how we can move forward.

32 See "Divestment: Faculty Members Make Their Case," *Harvard Magazine*, Oct. 14, 2014, harvardmagazine.com.

33 See Sustainability and Education Policy Network (SEPN), "The State of Fossil Fuel Development in Canadian Post-Secondary Institutions," Research Brief, Saskatoon, Sask., 2014.

34 Ibid.

35 Wade Davis, *The Wayfinders: Why Ancient Wisdom Matters in the Modern World* (Toronto: Anansi, 2009), pp.118–19.

36 Ibid., p.120.

37 Ibid.

38 Ibid., pp.121, 166, 167 (from the chapter "Century of the Wind").

EIGHT: Cleaning up the Mess

1 Kurt Vonnegut, *Slaughterhouse-Five* (New York: Delacorte, 1969).

2 Mary Mogan Edwards, "Ohio State Accuses 85 Students of Cheating on Online Tests," *Columbus Dispatch*, June 7, 2016.

3 Rick Seltzer, "Farewell to Departments," *Inside Higher Ed*, June 21, 2016.

4 Ibid.

5 Jack Stripling, "How George Mason Became Koch's Academic Darling," *The Chronicle of Higher Education,* May 13, 2016.

6 Matthew Barakat, "George Mason University Becomes a Favorite of Charles Koch," Associated Press, *The Big Story*, April 1, 2016.

7 Jake New, "Leaving the Big Time," *Inside Higher Ed*, April 29, 2016. Staben is quoted in the article.

8 Mike Herndon, "NCAA Study Finds All but 20 FBS Schools Lose Money on Athletics," Aug. 20, 2014, www.al.com.

9 New, "Leaving the Big Time."

10 Diana Mehta, "U.S. Plan to Draw Water from Great Lakes Approved, Raising Concerns in Canada," *The Star* (Toronto), June 21, 2016.

11 Ed Miliband, "The Inequality Problem," *London Review of Books* 38 (2016):3–4, 19–20. Miliband reviews three recent books on this matter: Anthony Atkinson, *Inequality: What Can Be Done?*; Joseph Stiglitz, *The Great Divide*; and Robert Putnam, *Our Kids: The American Dream in Crisis*.

12 Kentaro Toyama, "Why Technology Alone Won't Fix Schools," *The Atlantic*, June 2015, www.theatlantic.com.

13 Ibid.

Index